An Introduction to Rowing

By

IW Fourie, HL Fourie

Table of Contents

Introduction

Rowing, or crew as is it occasionally known in America, is a popular sport in the USA and internationally. This book is an introduction to the sport of rowing. The book covers the history, the basics of rowing, the types of boats, equipment, stroke technique, the handling and rigging of boats, the role of the coxswain, the different types of races, clubs and associations, and regattas. This book includes advice and tips for those who are new to the sport and want to quickly get an understanding of the details of rowing.

Rowing is a fun, enjoyable sport and is in fact one of the oldest competitive sports. Rowing is suitable for men and women of all ages. Rowing provides a challenge for a team in a crew of two, four or eight rowers, and for an individual in a single scull. Competitive rowing is regarded by exercise physiologists as one of the most physically demanding sports along with cross-country skiing and running. Rowing is one of the few sports where a novice can become a top class rower within a few years.

Rowing is a total body workout. To the casual spectator rowing looks only like an upper body sport. Although upper body strength is important, most of the power of the rowing stroke comes from the legs. Rowing is one of the few athletic activities that involve all of the body's major muscle groups. It is a great aerobic workout, in the same vein as cross-country skiing, and has the benefit of being a low-impact sport. As a competitive sport, rowing demands endurance, strength, balance, mental discipline, and an ability to continue on when your body is demanding that you stop.

The boats are also called shells because the hull is only about one quarter inch thick, so that it is as light as possible. In rowing all the rowers (except the coxswain) face away from the direction the boat is traveling, that is, they face the stern of the boat and not its bow.

There are two main types of rowing:

- Sweep boat rowing. Each rower has one oar held by both hands. The oar extends either to the starboard side or the port side of the boat. Since the forces are applied asymmetrically to the shell a sweep boat is more strongly constructed and is therefore heavier than a scull. Sweep boats have a rudder for steering.

- Sculling. Each rower has two oars, one in each hand. The oar itself is called a scull and is shorter than the oars used on a sweep boat. The boat is called a scull or a sculling boat, and the rower is called a sculler. Most sculls have no rudder and are steered by means of oar movements.

Although one may initially think that the rower is pulling an oar, in actuality the rower achieves most of the power by pushing the sliding seat towards the bow of the boat. Most of work is done by the legs and the upper back. The back should be kept straight from the hips to the shoulders. There is no bending at the waist which could lead to injury to the lower back.

This book is no substitute for actually being in a shell under the guidance and instruction of a qualified coach. There are many rowing clubs and associations throughout the world that welcome newcomers to the sport and provide coaching lessons and clinics. The Further Reading chapter has pointers to web sites that have contact information for many clubs and associations.

This book is divided into several chapters, organized by subject.

Chapter 1: History

This covers the fascinating history of rowing and describes how rowing has evolved from the transportation system of the old to the modern sport of rowing.

Chapter 2: Equipment

Here you will find descriptions of the boats, oars and other equipment used in rowing.

Chapter 3: Boat Handling

This chapter goes into the proper handling and rigging of boats.

Chapter 4: Sweep Rowing

This chapter introduces you to sweep rowing. The details of the stroke are described.

Chapter 5: Sculling

This chapter introduces you to sculling.

Chapter 6: Rowing Physiology

This chapter describes how the body consumes oxygen to generate the energy that is needed for rowing. The process of respiration and breathing are covered.

Chapter 7: Training

This chapter discusses training and the various drills tha can used to improve stroke technique.

Chapter 8: Coxing

This chapter covers the role and responsibilities of the coxswain. It also describes the commands and equipment that a coxswain will use.

Chapter 9: Races and Regattas

The different types of races are described in this chapter. These include sprints, head races and Bumps races. There is also a section on the more well known regattas.

Chapter 10: Clubs and Associations

This chapter lists some of the many rowing clubs and associations.

Chapter 11: Further Reading

This chapter lists the many reading resources that provide more background and detail on specific aspects of rowing as well as websites that provide information on equipment, clubs and associations.

There many other books that cover details on individual aspects of the sport in much more detail. The further reading chapter lists a selection of these books.

History

The Beginnings

In 1315 the Venice Regatta, the Regata Storica, was held for the first time. This regatta is still held today on the Grand Canal with races between different types of boats including the two-oared gondolino.

Figure 1: The River Thames with St. Paul's Cathedral on Lord Mayor's Day - Canaletto

There was competitive rowing between watermen who ferried passengers across the river Thames at London in small ferry barges called wherries. These competitions evolved to today's sport of rowing. In England oared barges were part of the Lord Mayor's water processions from 1454 until 1856. The oldest formal rowing event, Doggett's Coat and Badge, was first held in 1715 between apprentice English watermen who would provide ferry service across the Thames river. The Irish comedian, Thomas Doggett, offered an orange coat and a silver badge as a prize. The race is still rowed annually on the Thames.

Figure 2: Doggett's Coat and Badge

The race of 4 miles 5 furlongs (7,400 m) race is now held annually on the Thames between London Bridge and Cadogan Pier, Chelsea, passing under a total of 11 bridges.

Two eight-oared cutters, the Chatham and the Invincible, raced on the Thames from Westminster to Richmond on September 8 1788. This is the first boat race recorded in England's Annual Register and the Chatham won.

Europe

Amateur rowing started at Oxford University in 1815 and at Cambridge University a short while later. The oldest boat clubs in the world were founded about this time. These included the Leander Club, founded in 1818, Brasenose College Boat Club, Jesus College Boat Club and the Westminster School Boat Club, founded in 1813.

The first race between the Oxford and Cambridge universities was held in 1829, using professional watermen to coxswain their boats. The professionals were barred after the first race, and a highly formal code of amateurism has characterized English rowing ever since. Rowing is a gentleman's sport, with rules and behavior codes designed to encourage good sportsmanship.

The first French rowing club Societe Havraise de l'Aviron was established at Le Havre in 1838.

The Henley Regatta was established at a public meeting in the Town Hall, Henley-on-Thames, on March 26, 1839. In 1851, His Royal Highness Prince Albert became the first Royal Patron of the Regatta, and since then it has been called "Henley Royal Regatta." The Henley Royal Regatta is a social as well as athletic event, with most spectators decked out in formal finery. The Princess Elizabeth Cup is Henley's prize for the best schoolboy.

All rowing boats of this era had a fixed seat with oars mounted on the gunwales. This was called in-rigging. One of the first improvements was the use of outriggers to support the oars instead of having the oars in oarlocks mounted on the gunwale. This made the boat narrower with a smaller cross-section which reduced drag and so a boat with outriggers was be faster through the water. A type of outrigger was developed for racing boats by Anthony Brown of Newcastle-on-Tyne, England in 1828. Initially the riggers were wooden, but about 1841 Henry Clasper of Newcastle, England introduced a metal outrigger.

Another significant development was shell construction, with an internal frame with an external shell-like hull. In the 1870s the first shells were made from a type of papier-mâché.

The European Rowing Championships were first held in 1893 at Orta, Italy.

United States

The first races in the U.S.A. were between New York watermen who rowed passengers across the Hudson River. In 1756 a New York pettiauger defeated a Cape Cod whaleboat in a New York race. In 1811 two four-oared boats, the Knickerbocker and the Invincible, raced from Harsimus, New Jersey to the Battery, In 1823 the Knickerbocker Club became the first boat club organized in the United States. Club rowing started in New York Harbor in 1834 when the Castle Garden Amateur Boat Club Association was organized.

Seven eights and four sixes raced in a Philadelphia regatta in 1833.

Club rowing spread rapidly over the country as did club regattas and by 1872 there were more than 150 regattas throughout the United States. The Detroit Boat Club, founded in 1839 is the oldest club in the U.S.A. The Schuykill Navy, an association of amateur rowing clubs of Philadelphia was started in 1858 with most of the member clubs located on the Schuylkill River at the historic Boathouse Row. The Schuykill Navy was the first amateur sports organization in the U.S.A.

The first U.S. collegiate boat clubs were organized at Yale in 1843 and at Harvard the following year. Initially there was great variation in the types of boats used in intercollegiate rowing. There were six, eight and even ten oared shells, both with and without coxswain, and it was some years before the "eight" became the standard racing shell. The first intercollegiate athletic contest in the U.S.A. was a race of eight-oared boats from Harvard and Yale on Lake Winnepesaukee in 1852. An intercollegiate regatta between Brown, Harvard, Trinity and Yale boat clubs was planned in 1858, but then cancelled after the drowning of the Yale stroke. In 1871 Amherst, Brown, Bowdoin and Harvard formed the Rowing Association of American Colleges.

A major development in rowing technology was the sliding seat. In 1870 J.C. Babcock of New York City successfully fitted sliding seats to a Nassau Boat Club six. These were immediately popular in the U.S.A. and were used by Yale about a year later. They were used by Oxford and Cambridge universities in the 1873 Boat Race. This changed the sport as now the use of the powerful leg muscles added speed to the boats. In 1874 the swivel oar-lock was invented by Michael F. Davis of Portland, Maine.

In 1872 the National Association for Amateur Oarsmen was started for collegiate and amateur rowers.

Modern Era

FISA, the first international rowing sports federation, was founded in 1892.

Baron Pierre de Coubertin, founder of the modern Olympics, was a rower. Rowing at the first Olympic games in Athens in 1896 was cancelled due to bad weather, and the first Olympic rowing occurred in the second modern day Olympics at Paris in 1900. An eight from the Vesper Club of Philadelphia won the gold medal for the U.S. From 1920 to 1956 U.S. crews won the gold for the eights in every Olympics. The U.S. crews that won the eights included Navy in 1920 and 1952, Yale in 1924 and 1956, Cal-Berkeley in 1928, 1932 and 1948, and Washington in 1936.

In 1904, Hiram Conibear, an athletic trainer with no rowing experience, started a highly successful rowing program at the University of Washington. In 1911 the brothers George and Dick Pocock emigrated from England to Vancouver, British Columbia and started to build shells. George had sculled as a teenager in London and won the London Bridge to Chelsea race in 1910. In 1912 George Pocock was asked by Hiram Conibear to move to Seattle to build racing shells for the UW crew. The Pocock name soon became famous for well-crafted, race-winning shells. The UW eight won Olympic gold in Berlin in 1936 in a Pocock shell.

The first race between women's college eights took place in England between Cambridge's Newnham College Boat Club and the London School of Medicine for Women in 1919. The Women's Amateur Rowing Association was founded in England in 1923.

Jack Kelly of Philadelphia won gold medals single and double sculls in the 1920 Olympics in Antwerp and also a gold medal for single sculls in the 1924 Olympics in Paris. He was the father of Grace Kelly, the actress, and John Kelly who himself won a bronze medal for single sculls in the 1956 Olympics in Melbourne.

In 1953 Karl Adams founded the Ratzeburg Rowing Club at Ratzeburg, Germany. His innovative coaching and training techniques had a major impact on the development of rowing by introducing the use of interval training and weight training, as well as German rigging. The Ratzeburg eight won a gold medal at the 1960 Olympics in Rome, a silver medal at the 1964 Olympics in Tokyo, and a gold medal at the 1968 Olympics in Mexico.

In 1966 the first Head of the Charles was held in Cambridge, Massachusetts, and has grown to be the biggest regatta in the U.S.A.

For much of its history rowing has been a male dominated sport although women did participate at many levels. In 1954 women raced in the first international championship regatta for women at the European Championships on the Bosbaan in Amsterdam. The National Women's Rowing Association was formed in the early 1960's and in 1982 joined with the National Association for Amateur Oarsmen to become the United States Rowing Association. Women first participated in the 1976 Summer Olympics in Montreal. Internationally, women's rowing was dominated by Eastern European countries such as Russia, Bulgaria and Romania from the 50s until the 90s. The U.S.A. women's eight won their first Olympic gold medal in the 1984 games at Lake Casitas, California, and also won gold medals at the 2008 and 2012 Olympics.

Oars have evolved from the long symmetrical square ended oars used at the beginning of the 20th century to the shorter asymmetrical oars used today. In 1959 the wider tulip shaped oar become popular at the time of

European Rowing Championship held at Macon, France. The asymmetrical hatchet shaped blade, invented in 1992 by Peter and Dick Dreissigacker, is now widely used internationally.

Other improvements in equipment have happened in recent years with the introduction of new materials such as glass fiber, carbon fiber and Kevlar. The German company Empacher developed glass fiber boats at the time of the Munich Olympics in 1972. In 1977 the British company Carbocraft introduced carbon fiber shells which were much lighter than traditional wood constructed shells. They were soon popular in the U.S. Carbon fiber is also used for oars which are much lighter and without the tendency of wooden oars to warp. In addition, the heavier wooden oars tend to check the progress of the boat when they swing back on the recovery of a stroke.

A patent for a sliding rigger was registered by an English engineer in 1883. Development of the sliding rigger started after WWII using modern materials. In 1981 the German company Empacher built a rolling-rigger boat developed by Dr. Volker Notle. The rower Peter Michael Kolbe won the world sculling championship using this boat. However, use of sliding riggers has been banned by FISA. The great advantage of a sliding rigger is that since the rower's seat is fixed, the rower's mass is not moved fore and aft during the stroke which tends to check the progress of the boat. The French company Virus Boats manufactures boats using sliding riggers for recreational use.

In 1998 the River and Rowing Museum at Henley was opened. In 2000 Steve Redgrave of Great Britain had won gold medals in five consecutive Olympic games in pairs and fours.

Equipment

This chapter covers the equipment used in rowing. The different types of boats, oars and riggers are described. Also covered are the various measurements that are used to adjust and rig the boat properly.

Sweep Boats

In a sweep boat, each rower has one oar that is held by both hands. The oar extends either to the starboard side or the port side of the boat. Sweep boats have eight, four or two seats. All eights have a coxswain and boats with four and two seats may have seat for a coxswain or be coxless. Sweep boats are classified according to the number of rowers and the position of the coxswain. There are the following types of sweep boats:

- Eight (8+). This is a shell with eight seats and a coxswain. A coxswain is always needed because of the size of the boats. An eight is about 60 feet in length and has a weight of around 200 pounds.

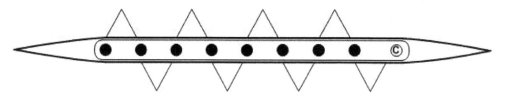

Figure 3: Eight (8+)

- Coxed Four (4+) and Coxless Four(4-). This is a shell with four rowers. A coxless four (4-) is also called a straight four and is commonly used by lightweight crews. A coxed four (4+) which is easier to row are usually used by school and club teams. A coxed four may be either bow-coxed (called a bow-loader) or stern-coxed. A coxed four is about 45 feet long and a coxless four about 44 feet long. They weigh about 110 pounds.

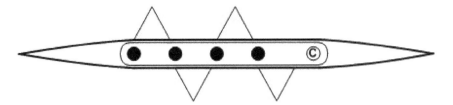

Figure 4: Coxed Four (4+)

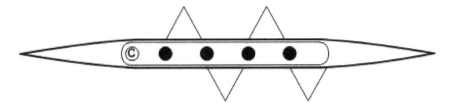

Figure 5: Bow-loader (4+)

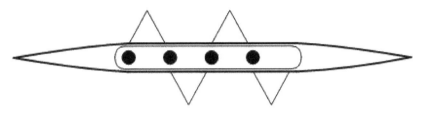

Figure 6: Coxless Four (4-)

- Coxed Pair (2+) and Coxless Pair (2-). This is a shell with 2 rowers. A coxless pair (2-) is also called a straight pair. Coxed pairs (2+) are rarely rowed by most club and school programs. A coxed pair is about 35 feet long and a coxless pair about 34 feet long. They weigh about 58 pounds.

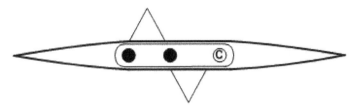

Figure 7: Coxed Pair (2+)

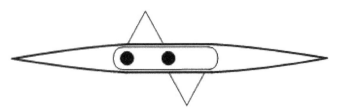

Figure 8: Coxless Pair (2-)

Sculls

In a scull, each rower has two oars, one in each hand, which extend to the starboard and port side of the boat. There are the following types of sculls:

- Quad (4x). This is a shell with four seats. This is about 42 feet in length and weighs about 110 pounds.

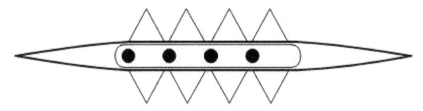

Figure 9: Quad (4x)

- Double (2x). This is a shell with two rowers. This is about 34 feet in length and weighs about 58 pounds.

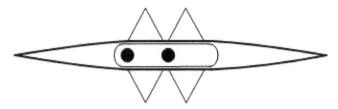

Figure 10: Double (2x)

- Single (1x). This is a shell with a single rower. This is about 27 feet in length, a foot wide and has a weight of about 30 pounds.

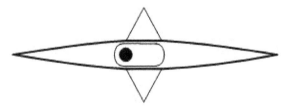

Figure 11: Single (1x)

Seats

Boats have sliding seats that run on tracks attached to the frame of the boat. Each seat has a set of four wheels that run on a pair of tracks as shown below. The tracks are also called rails. The pair of tracks is called a slide.

Figure 12: Seat and Slide

Seat Numbers

Seats are numbered sequentially from bow to stern. Number 1 seat is the bow seat and number 8 seat is the stroke seat. The port side of the boat is also called the stroke side since the stroke seat usually sits with the oar on the port side of the boat. The bow seat then has his oar on the starboard side of the boat and so this side is called the bow side.

Starboard (bow) side

Bow-four

Stern-four

Stroke seat

Bow

Stern

1 2 3 4 5 6 7 8

©

Bow seat   Bow-pair

Stern-pair

Port (stroke) side

← Direction of travel

Figure 13: Seat Numbering

Oars

An oar, also called a blade, is made of wood or carbon fiber. The oar has the following parts: the blade (or spoon), the shaft (or loom), the collar (or button) and the handle. Today, the cleaver shaped (or hatchet) blade, invented in 1992 by Peter and Dick Dreissigacker, is widely used. The asymmetric cleaver blade has been shown to be superior to the older Macon blade (also called the spoon or tulip oar) that was introduced in 1959. Prior to the Macon blade the longer square blade was used. The hatchet oar is shorter than a Macon oar since the surface of a hatchet blade is larger. Sculling oars are smaller than sweep oars.

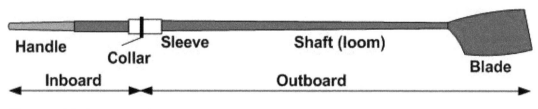

Handle   Collar   Sleeve   Shaft (loom)   Blade

Inboard   Outboard

Figure 14: Hatchet Oar

Figure 15: Macon Oar

Sweep boat oars are about 3.7 m (12 feet) long. Sculling oars are about 2.8 m (10 feet) long. A hatchet oar blade is about 55 cm long and 25 cm wide. The blade has a concave surface on the stern-facing side and a concave surface on the bow-facing side. The outboard length of an oar is measured from the tip of the blade to the outboard side of the collar.

The sleeve of the oar fits over the shaft where it passes through the oarlock and has a flat face to ensure that the oar blade is aligned at the right angle during the drive. The collar fits over the sleeve to prevent the oar from slipping out off the oarlock.

Figure 16: Sleeve and Collar of an Oar

The rubber grips on the handle of a sweep boat oar are shown below.

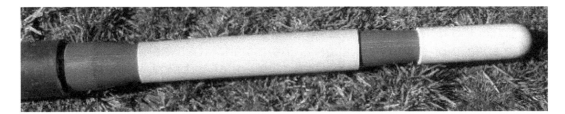

Figure 17: Sweep Boat Oar Handle

Gearing

Gearing is used to adjust the load of a oar in a similar way to the gears of a bicycle. The oar can be conveniently thought of as a mechanical lever with the fulcrum at the pin of the oarlock with the load being the resistance to forward motion through the oar blade, and the effort being the force applied by the rower at the oar handle. Gearing is the ratio of the distances of the load and the effort from the fulcrum.

Gearing = a / b

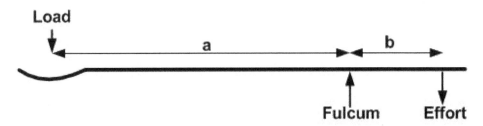

Since the points at which the load and effort are actually applied are not well defined, by convention the distance a is taken as the outboard length of an oar. Distance b is the span, which for a sweep boat, is the distance between the center of the oarlock pin and the centerline of the boat.

Increasing the gearing ratio has the effect of increasing the oar load and making the boat harder to row. Typically the gearing is not usually changed once set but can be altered by moving the collar on an oar, using oars with different length, or by using a different blade design such as hatchet oars instead of Macon oars. For a sweep boat the gearing ratio is about 3.1 and is higher than that of a scull since the rowers are dealing with one oar only. The gearing of a sweep boat is given by the equation:

Gearing = outboard length / span

= (overall oar length - inboard length) / span

For sculls the gearing is computed as the ratio of twice the outboard length to the span. For a scull the span is the distance between the oarlock pins. The gearing ratio of a scull is given by the equation below and usually has a value of about 2.5.

Gearing = 2 x outboard length / span

= 2 x (overall oar length - inboard length) / span

The gearing is adjusted by moving the collar inward or outward along the sleeve of the oar. The collar retaining clamp is loosened using a screwdriver and then collar is moved to an adjacent notch on the sleeve. The clamp is then tightened again. Moving the collar outward decreases the gearing and reduces oar load.

A CLAM or Clip-on Load Adjustment Method is a temporary shim that clips over the sleeve of an oar on the outboard side of the collar to reduce the gearing or load of an oar. Since the CLAM is between the collar and the oarlock, this increases the inboard length, decreases the outboard length and thereby reduces the gearing and makes the boat easier to row. A single CLAM has a width of 1 cm. It is convenient to use CLAMs when testing different oar loadings with a crew without having to come off the water to adjust the collars.

Riggers

Sweep boats are usually rigged with the riggers attached alternately to the port side then the starboard side from the stroke seat to the bow seat so that the stroke seat has the oar on the port side. Occasionally this may be reversed with the stroke seat having the oar to the starboard (bow) side to make use of a good starboard rower in the stroke seat. This is called bow rigging or starboard rigging.

The rigger consists of a frame and the oarlock. The rigger frame is bolted to the shell's gunwales. There are different types of riggers.

- Three-point rigger. This rigger has three points of attachment to the gunwale: the fore-stay, the main stay and the back stay.

- Two-point rigger. This rigger has two points of attachment to the gunwale: the main stay and the back stay.

- Wing rigger. A wing rigger that consists of an aluminum wing and a bracing strut called a backstay is shown below.

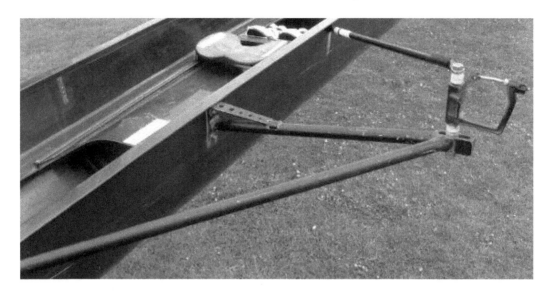

Figure 18: Three-point Rigger

Figure 19: Wing Rigger

It is the responsibility of the crew to rig the shell. Riggers are bolted to the gunwales using 7/16 inch hex-bolts in the USA and 11 mm hex-bolts in Europe. The picture below shows a starboard backstay and a port wing rigger bolted to the gunwale.

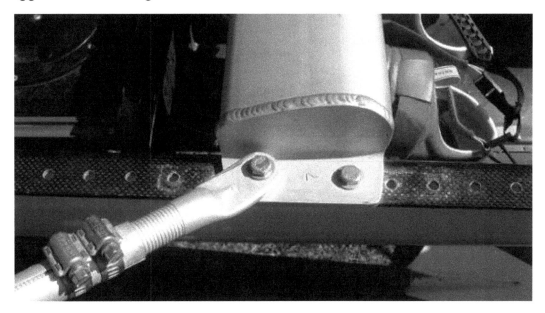

Figure 20: Rigger Attachment

A starboard wing rigger and backstay that have been detached from the shell are shown below.

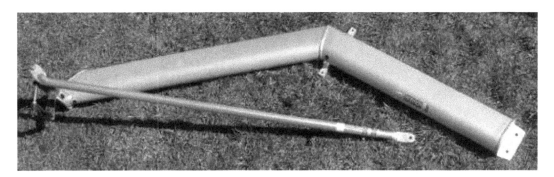

Figure 21: Wing Rigger

The oarlock actually holds the oar. The oarlock swivels on a pivot pin that is attached to the rigger frame. The oarlock is made up of the U-shaped swivel which rotates on the pin, the gate which is a metal bar that opens up to allow the oar to be inserted into the oarlock and a star locking nut at the end of the gate to ensure that the gate remains closed. Loosen the locking nut to open the gate, insert the sleeve of the oar into the oarlock, and then close the gate and tighten the locking nut.

Plastic pop-off shims can be snapped onto the pin below or above the swivel to adjust the height of the oarlock.

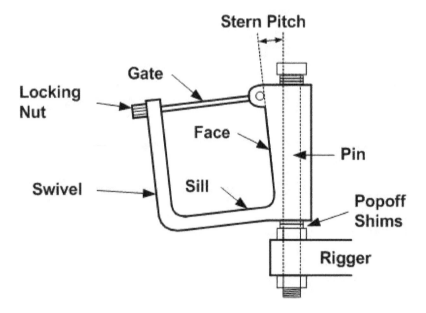

Figure 22: Oarlock Components

Figure 23: Oarlock

Rigger Dimensions

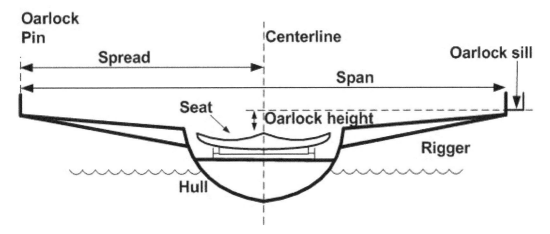

Figure 24: Rigger Dimensions

The spread is the distance from the centerline of the shell to the oarlock pin. It is measured by taking the distance between the outside of the port gunwale and the starboard gunwale, dividing by two, and then adding the distance from the outside of the gunwale to the center of the oarlock pin. The spread is about 81-88 cm. The picture of the oarlock above shows the spread measurement marked on the rigger.

On a scull, the span is the distance between the port oarlock pin and the starboard oarlock pin. The span is about 157-161 cm. On a scull the starboard oarlock is rigged 1-2 cm higher than the port oarlock so that the left hand is above the right hand at the crossover point.

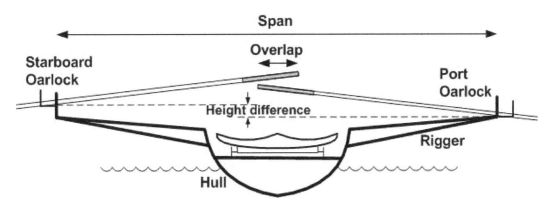

Figure 25: Oarlock height on Scull

The oarlock height is the distance from the oarlock sill to the top of the seat. This is usually about 13-19 cm. To measure the oarlock height, place a straight edge or spirit level across the gunwales. Then use a tape measure to get the distance from the oarlock sill (the bottom of the oarlock) to the straight edge, and then from the straight edge to the top of the seat.

During the drive, the working face of the sleeve of the oar is driven hard against the face of the oarlock and so the angle of the oarlock face sets the stern pitch to the oar blade. There are two pitch measurements:

- Stern pitch. This is the tilt of the blade of the oar during the drive from the perpendicular towards the stern. This ensures that the blade does not dive too deep during the drive. However if the stern pitch is too large the blade will tend to slip out of the water. Stern pitch is about 4 - 7 degrees and can be measured with a pitch meter (or pitch gauge). The actual pitch of the blade includes the pitch of the oarlock and the pitch of the blade itself. In the US most oar blades have zero pitch, so that the blade of the oar is parallel to flat face of the sleeve, unless the oar is warped. To measure the stern pitch of the oarlock place the pitch meter against the face of the oarlock when it is in the mid-drive position (the oarlock swivel is parallel to the centerline of the boat).

- Lateral pitch. This is also called outboard pitch. This is the tilt of the oarlock pin away from the centerline of the shell. Lateral pitch is about 0-1 degree and cannot usually be changed.

Stern pitch can be changed by making adjustments to the oarlock, or by using an oar with a different pitch. The diagram below shows the sleeve of the oar against the working face of the oarlock. The angle of the working face of an oarlock can be adjusted by inserting different pitch bushings between the oarlock pin and the swivel. Oarlock manufacturers provide rigging manuals that describe the details of how to do this.

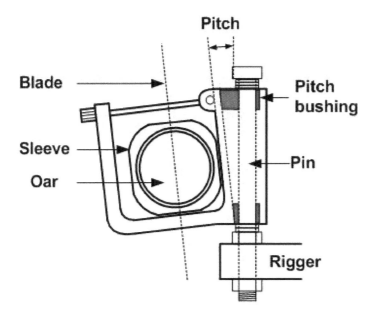

Figure 26: Oarlock Pitch

Another important aspect to the attachment of riggers to the shell is Work-through or "Work-through the pin". Work-though is how far a rower's seat is rigged in front of the oarlock pin and is measured as the distance from the front edge of the seat at the catch position to the pin of the oarlock. On a scull this can be done by tying a string between the two pins of the oarlocks and measuring the distance the front of the seat moves further towards the catch position from the line of the string. Work-through varies from 0 to 2 cm for pairs, to 8 to 12 cm for eights.

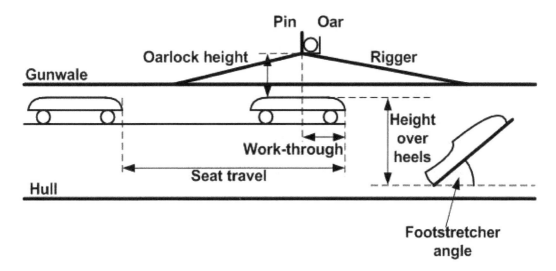

Figure 26: Side view showing Work-through

Increasing Work-through will allow greater compression of the legs at the catch resulting in increased propulsion at the start of the drive. This will increase the catch angle which is the angle of the oar when it enters the water. The catch angle is measured from an imaginary line perpendicular to the centerline of the boat. Work-through may be adjusted by attaching the rigger further towards the bow or stern, or by moving the tracks of the seat. If these adjustments are made it may also be necessary to change the fore and aft position of the footstretcher so that the rower's seat does not hit the front stops of the slide at the catch position, and the rear stops of the slide at the release position.

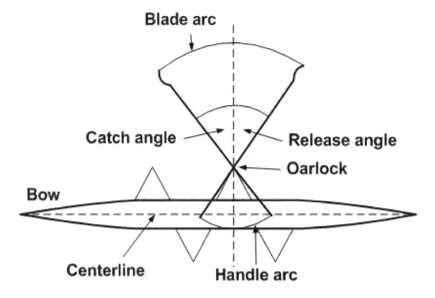

Figure 27: Catch angle

Rigger Attachment

The method of attaching riggers alternately to the port side and then the starboard side from the stroke seat to the bow seat is known as standard rigging. However, on eights and fours the riggers may also be attached to a shell in what is called tandem rigging. There are two types of tandem rigging: German (bucket) rigging and Italian rigging as shown in the diagram below. The advantage of tandem rigging is that the forces that cause yaw or wiggle during the stroke cancel out and this leads to less resistance to forward motion and improved rowing efficiency.

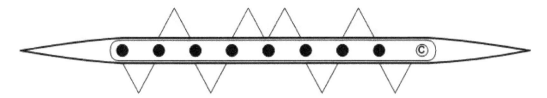

Figure 28: German Rigged Eight

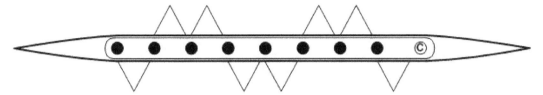

Figure 29: Italian Rigged Eight

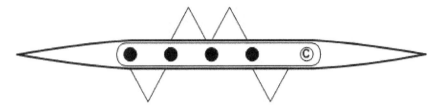

Figure 30: Italian Rigged Four

The rigger bolts are tightened and loosened using a 7/16 inch or 11 mm box-wrench or ring-spanner, also called a rigger jigger. Always use the box (ring) end of the rigger-jigger as the open end may slip off the bolt head and damage the hull.

Footstretcher

The footstretcher is an inclined footrest that holds the rower's shoes. The rower places his feet into the shoes attached to the footstretcher. The height, angle and position of the footstretcher may be adjusted.

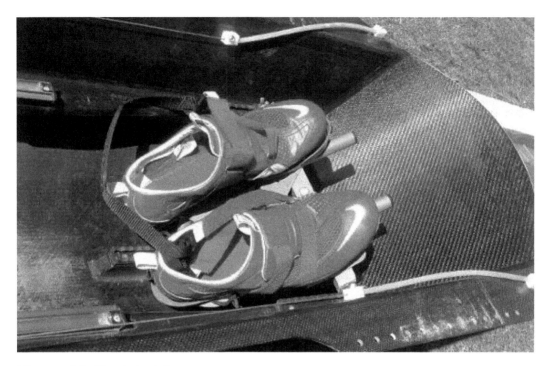

Figure 31: Footstretcher

The height of the footstretcher (also called height over heels) is the vertical distance from the lowest point of the seat to the lowest point of the heel of the footstretcher. The height of the footstretcher should be such that the rower's shoulders are above the knees so the arms can reach forward comfortably at the catch position. This height is usually about 14 - 20 cm. To measure the footstretcher height, place a straightedge or spirit level across the gunwales of the boat, measure the distance from the bottom of the straightedge to the heel of the footstretcher. Then subtract the distance from the bottom of the straightedge to the lowest point of the seat.

The angle of the footstretcher is between footboard and the horizontal. The angle should be such that the rower's heels remain down against the footstretcher throughout the stroke. A footstretcher angle of between 38 and 45 degrees should ensure that the rower has comfortable foot placement.

The fore and aft position of the footstretcher may be adjusted to set the desired Work Through as mentioned in the previous section on riggers. The footstretcher should be adjusted towards the bow if the rower is hitting the front stops of the slide when at the catch position, and towards the stern if the rower is hitting the back stops of the slide when at the release position.

Rudder

The rudder is attached to the skeg (or fin) that protrudes from the stern-end of the keel. The rudder is controlled by the coxswain using attached cables. The skeg and the rudder are shown below.

Figure 32: Rudder and Skeg

The rudder is steered by the coxswain or by one of the rowers in a coxless boat. In a coxless boat the rudder cables are connected to one of the footstretchers and is controlled by the rower moving the ball of their foot in the starboard or port direction. This is called toe-steering. The steering cables are crossed to enable this to happen. The picture below shows the control yoke for the rudder and its steering cables.

Figure 33: Rudder Control Yoke and Cables

The picture below shows the steering cables used by the coxswain.

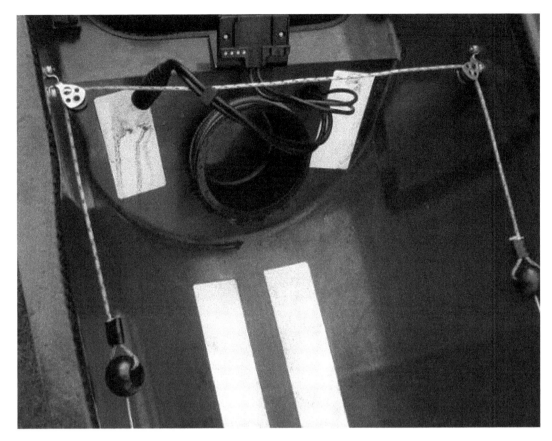

Figure 34: Steering Cables

Is it important to note that effect of the rudder is not immediate and usually takes a few strokes before the boat starts to turn. It is better to under steer by making small adjustments, rather than to over steer and have to make corrections in the other direction.

Rowing Machines

Indoor rowing machines are also called Ergometers or Ergs. Rowing machines consist of a flywheel with a set of vanes that impel air to simulate a load, a drive cord and a handle. They have a fixed footstretcher and a sliding seat mounted on a rail. There is also a damper or braking mechanism which impedes air flow through the vanes of the flywheel and can be used to adjust the stroke rate that the rower can achieve.

Figure 35: Rowing machine

Indoor rowing machines provide the rower a means to get excellent cardiovascular exercise off the water and also help improve stroke technique. The rower should use the same rowing technique as for rowing a shell. The drive should have the same sequence of using the legs, torso and then the arms as described in detail in the chapters on sweep rowing and sculling. It is an efficient workout making it possible to burn in excess of 1000 Kilocalories per hour. A typical workout would consist a steady piece for 20 to 40 minutes.

Rowing machines also have a digital readout so that the rower can measure the stroke rate in strokes per minute (SPM) and also the distance covered. There is also a conversion from Split Time to power measurements in Watts or Kilocalories per hour.

The damper is used to adjust how quickly the force from the handle is applied to the machine. A higher damper setting will result in a slower stroke rating, while a lower damper setting will result in a faster stroke rating.

Although a rowing machine is a great way to exercise it is not a substitute for actual time on the water. One characteristic of boat behavior that a rowing machine does not provide is that of lateral tilt; the rower needs to be able to balance a boat.

Concept2 is by far the most popular manufacturer of Erg machines.

Measurements

Erg machines have several measurements that can be used to improve the rower's stroke and power.

- Stroke Rate. This is the rower's cadence or number of strokes per minute (SPM). During training this should between 18 and 30. In a race this is typically 30-40 SPM. During a Power-10 the stroke rate is about 40 SPM.

- Split Time. This is average time to row 500 m and is labelled av/500m on a rowing machine. This is an indication of the power of each stroke, in other words how hard the rower has pulled. It does not correspond to how many strokes the rower takes since strokes can vary in power. The Split Time can be converted to power measurements such as KiloCalories per hour or Watts.

The digital display for a typical rowing machine is shown below.

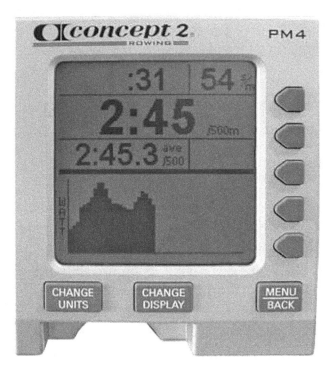

Figure 36: Rowing machine display

Stretching

A rowing workout should be preceded by some stretching exercises. Before stretching perform a short 3-5 minute easy row to warm up the muscles. Stretching helps to keep the muscles supple and prepares them for the activity. It also helps maintain full range of motion for the muscles, release tension in the muscles, develop body awareness and promote circulation.

Each stretch should be done in a slow, relaxed fashion without any abrupt motion and held for about 30 seconds. For single sided stretches repeat on each side. These should include stretches of the lower back, back of the leg, and shoulders.

Here are some good stretches:

- To stretch the quadriceps muscles, while standing pull your foot backwards and up bending the knee.

- To stretch the hamstring muscles, while sitting on the floor move your hands forward along the leg toward the toes, leaning and bending from the waist while keeping your back straight.

- Torso rotation. Lie on your back, bend your hip and knee to 90 degrees, place your opposite hand on the knee while keeping the opposite leg extended straight, then pull your knee and leg across the center of the body, turn your head toward the opposite side and your extend arm.

- To stretch the posterior rotator cuff and shoulder, stand with your arm in front of you, use the opposite hand to hold underneath your arm just above the elbow and then slowly pull your arm across your body toward the opposite shoulder.

- To stretch the gastrocnemius, soleus, and achilles tendon of the lower leg, stand facing a wall and separate your feet with one leg bent closer to the wall. With elbows straight lean forward with your hands on wall. The calf muscles of the leg further from the wall are then stretched.

Workouts

Workouts should always start with a short 3-5 minute piece of easy rowing to warm up, followed by stretching exercises. After stretching various workout pieces can be used such as:

Four 5-minute pieces varying the stroke rate: 20, 22 and 24 SPM, with 1 minute easy rowing in between.

Two 10-minute pieces at a steady stroke rate: 20-24 SPM with 2 minutes easy rowing in between.

Single 30-60 minute piece at a varying stroke rate: 20-24 SPM.

Finally do 3-5 minutes of easy rowing to cool down, followed by stretching exercises.

Boat Handling

Boats are fragile and easily damaged so they need to be lifted, carried and maneuvered with care. Proper boat handling is required to ensure that the shells can be taken to the water, removed from the water, and returned to their racks in the boathouse without being damaged or causing injury to anyone. Boats will also need to be de-rigged for transport on boat trailers. The coxswain has a key role in directing all boat handling activities.

Oars should always be carried with the blades in front of you so you can see where they are and avoid getting them damaged.

Carrying the Boat

An eight weighs about 200 pounds so it important that the crew lift the boat together so that any individual does not lift more weight than necessary. The coxswain must check that all crew members are present and ready before lifting by calling a roll-call count down. The coxswain should usually walk near the stern to watch the skeg and ensure that it is not damaged. To lift the shell from a rack and carry it out of the boathouse this procedure should be followed:

1. Each rower should stand next to a seat.

2. When the coxswain calls "Hands on", each rower will reach across to the opposite gunwale and wait.

3. When the coxswain calls "Ready, up and out", the rowers in unison lift the shell off the rack and out into the middle of the boathouse.

4. The coxswain then instructs the rowers separate alternately to each side of the boat with the command "Split to shoulders" or "Split to waists" to carry the boat out of the boathouse.

5. On the command "Walk it out" the crew walk forward carrying the boat out of the boathouse. The coxswain should call "Watch the riggers" on moving past the doors.

Boats are usually carried upside down but may be canted to the side in some situations. Eights and fours should be carried with each rower having the gunwale opposite their rigger on their shoulder, or at waist height with arms extended.

Shells may be carried by the crew from the boathouse to an open area where they can be seated on two boat slings for rigging. For an eight, the slings should be placed under the two and seven seat rigging. For a four shell, the slings should be placed under the one and four seat rigging.

Figure 38: Boat Sling

Then once rigged the shell can be carried to the dock.

Figure 37: Lowering a boat onto slings

Getting into the Boat

The following steps should be used to get into the boat once it is in the water. Assuming the port-side is against the dock.

1. Stroke-side rowers put their oars in and close the gates and hold the boat.

2. Bow-side rowers get in with their oars and put them in the gates.

3. After bow-side oars are pushed out the stroke-side rowers get in.

4. The coxswain gets in.

Getting out of the Boat

After rowing a similar procedure is followed for getting out of the boat. Assuming the bow-side rowers have their blades on the dock.

1. The coxswain gets out.

2. Bow-side rowers get out and hold the boat.

3. Stroke-side rowers undo their gates, get their oars and get out.

4. Bow-side rowers get their oars out.

In the Boat

There are several aspects to rowing that someone new to rowing needs to be aware of. These include the balance of the boat, steering and stroke technique. These will be covered in the next few sections.

Balance

The balance or set of a boat is a key part of rowing. Each rower should ideally have their weight directly over the centerline of the boat. However, sweep boat rowing requires that the weight of a rower deviate slightly from being directly the centerline, particularly at the catch. Starboard side rowers will lean slightly to starboard at the catch, and port side rowers will lean slightly to port at the catch. Part of the balance of the boat is making sure all rowers in the boat do this at the same time so that the torque to starboard and port is balanced.

As a new rower, take easy strokes to internalize proper rowing technique and do not focus on maximizing power. Balance is one of the most difficult things to achieve in rowing, so do not feel bad if the boat rocks a lot at first. One of the first things a novice learns is how to balance the boat the oars flat on the surface of the water.

Steering

The boat is steered by the coxswain in the case of coxed boats. The coxswain should always scan ahead of the boat, be alert for other boats and potential obstacles and steer to avoid them. Correct steering in head races is important since these are normally on long winding riverine courses. The coxswain must steer a line that will minimize the time but also avoid any buoys and other riverside obstacles. The coxswain should take note of any landmarks when rowing to the starting line.

The coxswain should be aware of wind conditions. The coxswain will need to make small steering adjustments to counter a cross wind during a race. In the case of a cross wind a lane assignment that is on the lee side of other boats would have an advantage.

Steering can be done using the rudder when the shell is moving and using the oars when the shell is in motion or stationary.

Steering using Rudder

Rudder is the most usual method when making gradual turns while the shell is in motion. If the coxswain's cockpit is in the stern, the rudder is controlled by a cable that runs along the edge of the cockpit as shown in Figure 34. There may be two small rubber balls connected into the cable on the starboard and port side to help judge the amount of turn. The starboard and port rudder control cables should be held lightly in each hand between the thumb and forefinger. Move one of the cables towards the bow to turn the shell in that direction. For example, to steer to port move the port side cable forward. The coxswain should test the rudder movement when the boat is out of the water before starting any rowing session.

The coxswain should steer by aiming at a distant point and making small adjustments towards that point. It is better to under steer towards the aiming point rather than to over steer and have the boat fishtail towards the target.

Steering may be done during the recovery or during the drive, and to achieve the desired amount of turn the rudder movement may need to be applied over several strokes. Steering during the recovery is most responsive because the boat is fastest at this time. However, since the blades are out of the water during the recovery the boat is at its most unstable state and big movements of the rudder will affect the balance of the boat. The smaller rudder movement will result in less drag and so this method is usually preferred during a race.

Steering during the drive is less responsive but has the advantage that the boat is more stable. The disadvantage of this method is that the rudder movement will need to be applied over more strokes to achieve the same turning effect resulting in more drag.

Steering using Oars

When the shell is in motion, steering can also be done by added or reduced pressure on the starboard or port oars. This may also be used when sharper turns need to be negotiated. For example, the coxswain would call "port pressure" to start a turn to starboard and then "even pressure" to stop the added pressure.

The shell can also be turned using squared oars on the starboard or port side. This will check the boat on the side that the oars are squared causing it to turn in that direction. For example, the coxswain will call "Stroke hold water" to get the stroke to square his oar to make a turn to port.

Since the rule of passing is to navigate around a body of water by keeping the bank close to the starboard side of the boat, boats will typically need to make turns to port. To do this the coxswain will call "Port back" and "Starboard row".

When the shell is stationary, it can also be turned by taking backing strokes or rowing in the reverse direction. This is typically used when maneuvering the boat when docking or when lining the boat up at the start of a sprint race.

When the shell is stationary, it can be turned to starboard by getting seat 2 to take a one or more strokes. To turn more sharply, seats 2 and 4 can take strokes. This will also cause the shell to move forward. To rotate the shell in place in a clockwise direction, seat 2 should take some strokes while seat 7 does backing strokes.

The shell can be turned to port by getting bow seat to take a one or more strokes. To turn more sharply, bow seat and seat 3 can take strokes. To rotate the shell in place in a counter clockwise direction, the bow seat should take some strokes while the stroke seat does backing strokes.

The coxswain may decide to use both the rudder and added or reduced oar pressure in certain situations.

Sweep Rowing Technique

In a sweep boat the rowers have theirs oars extending to the starboard or port side of the shell. Novice rowers should try rowing both starboard and port positions to determine their preference and aptitude.

Holding the Oar

The hand closest to the rigger is called the inside hand and the hand furthest from the rigger is the outside hand. When rowing at port the left hand is the outside hand, and when rowing at starboard the right hand is the outside hand.

The Stroke

Rowing is a cycle of repeated strokes. Each stroke consists of four steps during which the seat slides between two positions: closest to the stern and closest to the bow.

1. The Catch is the instant at which the oar blade is placed in the water and the drive starts. The seat is at a position closest to the stern.

2. The Drive is when the oar blade is in the water and the rower is pulling on the oar. The rower drives the seat towards the bow by extending the legs.

3. The Release (also called the Extraction or the Finish) is the instant at the end of the drive when the oar blade is removed from the water. The seat is at a position closest to the bow.

4. The Recovery is when the oar is out of the water and the rower is moving the seat back to Catch position.

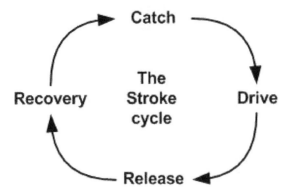

Figure 40: The Stroke Cycle

It is important to note that although the phases of the stroke have been identified and described here, when actually rowing the stroke must be a smooth, continuous movement from one phase of the stroke to the next and from one stroke to the next.

The Drive

The rower starts the drive at the catch position with seat at the stern-most position with the knees bent and legs compressed with the arms extended towards the stern. The shins of the leg should be vertical, the chest resting on thighs, arms straight and the rower's weight on the balls of the toes. The rower's head should be up and be looking beyond the stern of the boat. Avoid looking down into the shell as this will cause the chin to drop and the back to be rounded. The rower's back should be erect and slightly pivoted forward. The outside shoulder should be slightly rotated towards the rigger and should be slightly higher than the inside shoulder. The outside arm will be between the rower's knees so they should be a natural distance apart. The body position is shown below.

Figure 41: Body Position at the Catch

At the catch the rower places the oar blade into the water by rapidly raising the arms by pivoting them up straight-armed from the shoulders, and then starts to extend the legs to push the seat towards the bow of the boat. This applies pressure on the oar blade to drive the boat forward through the water. The drive may be broken into three sequential phases:

First, the rower extends the legs to push the seat towards the bow. This is called the leg drive. Most of the power for the stroke comes from this strong leg extension. There is no pivot of the back or bending the arms. The rower's back angle should be unchanged for the first half of the drive. The shoulder muscles should not be engaged, the arms should be extended forward as if hanging from the oar.

Next, the rower leverages the torso backwards towards the bow as the legs near full extension. The pivot of the torso toward the bow should occur during the last quarter of the leg drive. The body position as the rower starts to lean backwards is shown below.

Figure 42: Body Position at the Half Slide

Finally, the rower draws the arms towards the chest when the torso has passed vertical. The hands should almost touch the chest just above the diaphragm and have enough room to drop to remove the blades from the water for the release. The body position at the Release is shown below.

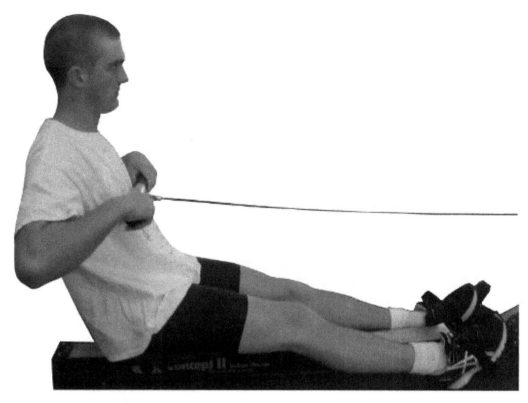

Figure 43: Body Position at the Release

This sequence is important because the muscle groups of the body used in the stroke: the legs, the back and the arms, have decreasing strength. The most powerful muscle group, the legs are used first, followed by a transition to the pivot of the back towards the bow, and finally the arms. The handle and seat should move together during the drive.

The Recovery

The rower starts the recovery by pushing down on the oar handle to lift the blade from the water at the release. The oar blade should come out of the water perpendicular to the surface of the water. Once the blade is out of the water the rower starts to feather the oar so that the blade of the oar is parallel to the surface of the water. The recovery may also be broken into three sequential phases:

First, the rower extends the arms out in front. This is the arms-away position shown in the picture below.

Figure 44: Arms-away Body Position

Next, the rower leans the torso forward. The boat reaches its maximum velocity through the water.

Finally, when the torso is just past vertical, the rower starts to bend the knees which causes the seat to move towards the stern of the boat. The oar handle must be past the knees before they break. This bending of the knees occurs slightly more slowly than the drive and allows the rower a moment to recover. The boat now merely glides through the water.

The recovery completes with the seat moving toward the stern position and the legs compressing until the shins are vertical again. The shins should be vertical and aligned with the feet and not flared outward. It is important to achieve maximum leg compression in each stroke since the bulk of the power for the stroke comes from leg extension during the next drive.

The recovery phase of the stroke is performed more slowly than the drive, in fact only about a third of the time for the whole stroke cycle is used for the drive and two thirds is used for the recovery. This gives the rower a chance to rest and prepare for the next drive. The rowing ratio is the ratio of the time spent on the drive versus the time for the recovery. The value of the ratio should about 0.5, meaning that about twice time is spent during the recovery compared with the drive. The goal is to have a powerful drive followed by a relaxed recovery without rushing forward up the slide.

In summary the stroke is a repeated cycle as follows: catch, legs, back, arms, release, arms, back, legs. The stroke should represent power under graceful control with the minimum of splashing as the oar blade enters and leaves the water.

Feathering

Feathering is done during the recovery phase of the stroke when the oar blade is out of the water. When feathered the blade of the oar is parallel to the surface of the water (with the face of the blade facing upwards) so that it meets less wind resistance and is able to slice through the air during the recovery. During the drive the wrists should be straight with the arms.

Feathering starts when the rower drops the hands to remove the blade from the water and most of the blade is out of the water. In sweep rowing, the rower rotates the inside wrist backwards as the arms are being extended. This will twist the oar such that the blade rotates from being perpendicular (or square) to being parallel to the surface of the water. The outside wrist remains straight with the outside arm.

As the recovery phase completes, the rower squares the blade just as the hands are over the ankles. The inside wrist is rotated forward to normal position to square the blade in readiness for the catch.

The diagram below shows the feathering of a blade during a stroke.

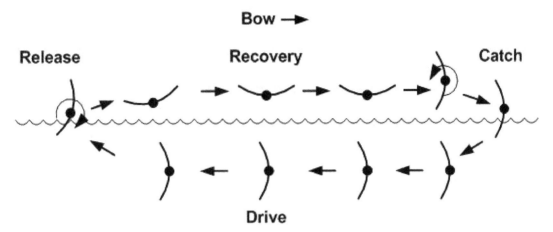

Figure 45: Feathering

Anatomy of the Stroke

The diagram below shows the change in instantaneous velocity of the boat during a stroke from a minimum near the start of the drive to a maximum during the recovery. Also shown are the phases of the stroke as well as the catch and release points. Notice that the recovery takes a longer time than the drive.

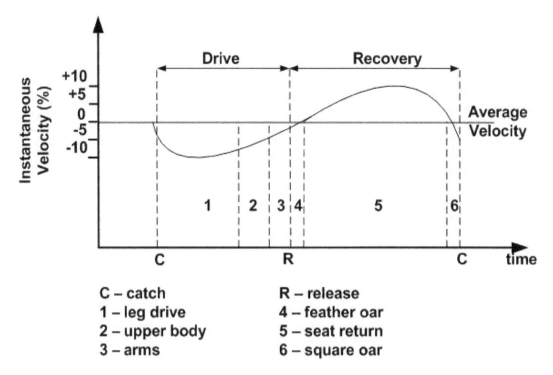

C – catch   R – release
1 – leg drive   4 – feather oar
2 – upper body   5 – seat return
3 – arms   6 – square oar

Figure 46: Velocity Profile

The diagram below shows the stance of the rower at the various phases of the stroke.

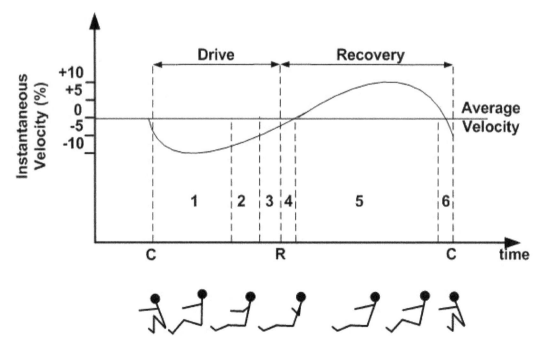

Figure 45: Stroke Stance

Mistakes in the Stroke

Here is a list of common mistakes in the stroke:

1. Incorrect posture. The rower's back should ideally be as straight as possible. The rower should sit up tall with the head up and looking beyond the stern of the boat.

2. Lifting shoulders during the drive. The shoulders should be level through the drive and move through a horizontal plane.

3. Rowing with bent arms. The rower should hang from the oar with straight arms for the first part of the drive. Rowing with bent arms will result in the rower exerting unnecessary effort.

4. Rowing with bent wrists. After feathering the wrists should be straight with the arm.

5. Over reaching at the catch.

6. Pivoting the torso backwards too early in the drive which will be seen as the handle moving first before the seat.

7. Leaning back too much and drawing the handle too high.

8. Rushing the slide. This is moving the seat forward too quickly during the recovery. The time taken on the recovery should be about twice the time spent on the drive.

9. Shooting the slide. This is pushing the lower back out at the beginning of the drive ahead of the upper body. The body should be in about the same one o'clock stance as at the catch until the body starts to lean back.

10. Breaking the knees too early on the recovery. This will result in the hands having to lift up over the knees.

11. Not being relaxed.

12. Not maintaining adequate pressure on the foot stretcher.

13. Thumping the handle into the chest at the finish. The hands should not touch the chest at the finish.

Teamwork and Coordination

Rowing is all about teamwork. The rowers of all sweep boats and double and quad sculls must perform the stroke in a coordinated fashion. If this is not done the boat will be "checked" and its progress slowed. Timing must be coordinated and all the rowers must perform the catch simultaneously so that the whole stroke is carried out in unison. Each rower must watch the rower immediately in front and the stroke sets the cadence.

Manoeuvring the boat

The crew must be able to manoeuvre the shell in all situations such as when leaving and returning to the dock, or lining up at the start of a race. The coxswain will call the commands to perform these operations. The boat can be moved around by using individual rowers or groups of rowers. To move forward or backward slowly, the coxswain may use the "bow pair", "stern pair", "bow four" or "stern four".

The coxswain may call "Bow pair back it", or "Port/starboard back it" depending on whether it is a backing up or turning manoeuvre. To do the backing stroke the rower sits with legs extended and puts the oar blades into the water and pushes the oar handle forward and then pivots the torso forward. When the arms are fully extended the rower drops the arms to remove the oar from the water, pivots the torso backwards and pulls the oar handle back to the chest. This backing stroke is repeated until the coxswain calls "Weigh enough".

Sculling Technique

The stroke for sculling is similar to rowing but there is the difference of having to control two oars.

Handling a Single Scull

A single scull is light enough for a rower to be able to carry it from the boathouse to the dock without the aid of someone else. Hold the scull by the gunwales and then lift it off the rack to an overhead position and rest one gunwale on the left shoulder. Hold one rigger by the left hand and a point forward of where the gunwale rests on the shoulder with the right hand, so that the shell has three separated points of contact with the body. The rower can now walk to the dock. Watch the riggers so they do not collide the doors, trees and anyone else. At the dock lower the scull to the waist and then slowly place it into the water. Make sure the all porthole covers and water-tight seals are closed.

To get into a single scull once it is in the water beside the dock follow the procedure described below. This assumes that the starboard side of scull is against the dock.

1. Put the oars in the oarlocks. Place the narrow part of the oar shaft at the blade end into the oarlock, then slide the oar out through the oarlock until the button touches the oarlock. Tighten the gate nuts.

2. Undo the Velcro straps on the shoes of the footstretcher.

Sit on the dock next to seat of the scull facing the stern with legs bent and feet just to the bow side of the starboard rigger.

3. Put your left hand on the dock and your right hand on the port-side deck between the seat and the port gunwale. Make sure your left hand, your body, the seat and right hand are in a line.

4. With your weight on each arm, hoist yourself from the dock onto the seat.

5. Hold the oars with the right hand.

6. Put your feet into the stretcher's shoes and close the straps with the left hand. Another way to close the straps is to put both oar handles into the armpits with blades resting on the water, and then extend the arms over the

handles to reach the stretcher, by sliding forward on the seat so that the oar handles are positioned between the thighs and arms.

7. Push off from the dock with the left hand using a good strong shove.

8. Take the oars in each hand.

9. Start to row slowly away from the dock.

Getting out a single scull on return to the dock is essentially the reverse of the procedure described above.

The oars should be held with the thumbs on the end of the oar handles to keep the oars snug against the oarlocks. The rower should have control over both oar handles at all times to maintain the balance of the scull. The oar blades act as outriggers that prevent the scull from rolling over as long as they are held by the rower. Once rowing, the rower (the bow seat in a double or a quad) should look back over their shoulder every five or strokes to check the direction of the scull along the course.

The Stroke

Each stroke consists of the same four steps described for sweep rowing.

1. The Catch is the instant at which both oar blades are placed in the water and the drive starts. The seat is at a position closest to the stern.

2. The Drive is when both oar blades are in the water and the rower is pulling on the oars. The rower drives the seat towards the bow by extending the legs.

3. The Release is the instant at end of the drive when both oar blades are removed from the water. The seat is at a position closest to the bow.

4. The Recovery is when the oars are out of the water and the rower is moving back to Catch position.

The starboard and port oar handles overlap in the middle of the drive and recovery. This is the crossover point. The starboard (to the rower's left) oarlock is rigged slightly higher (1-2 cm) than the port and so the rower must row with the left hand slightly higher than the right, so that at the middle of the drive and recovery the starboard handle is directly over the port handle. The starboard oarlock is raised by inserting a plastic snap-on (pop-off) shim onto the pin below the oarlock.

The Drive

The rower starts the drive at the catch position with seat at the stern-most position with the knees bent and legs compressed with the arms extended towards the stern. The shins of both legs should be vertical. The rower's head is up and should be looking beyond the stern of the boat with the torso erect and slightly pivoted forward. The rower's shoulders should be level and remain so throughout the stroke.

At the catch the rower places the oar blades into the water by rapidly raising the arms and then starts to extend the legs to push the seat towards the bow of the boat. This applies pressure on the oar blades to drive the boat forward through the water. The drive may be broken into three sequential phases:

First, the rower extends the legs to push the seat towards the bow. Most of the power for the stroke comes from the leg extension.

Second, the rower leans the torso towards the bow as the legs near full extension.

Finally, the rower draws the arms towards the chest. The hands should almost touch the chest just above the diaphragm and have enough room to drop to remove the blades from the water for the extraction.

The Recovery

The rower starts the recovery by pushing down on the oar handles to lift the blades from the water at the release. The oar blades should come out of the water perpendicular to the surface of the water. Once the blades are out of the water the rower starts to feather the oars so that the blades are parallel to the surface of the water. The recovery may also be broken into three sequential phases:

First, the rower extends the arms out in front. This is the arms-away position.

Next, the rower leans the torso forward. The boat reaches its maximum velocity through the water.

Finally, when the torso is just past vertical, the rower starts to bend the knees and this causes the seat to move towards the stern of the boat. The oar handle must be past the knees before they bend. This bending of the knees occurs slightly more slowly than the drive and allows the rower a moment to recover. The boat now merely glides through the water.

The recovery completes with the seat moving toward the stern position and the legs compressing until the shins are vertical again. It is important to achieve maximum leg compression in each stroke since the bulk of the power for the stroke comes from leg extension during the next drive.

The recovery is performed more slowly than the drive to give the rower a chance to rest and prepare for the next drive.

Feathering

Feathering is done during the recovery phase of the stroke when the oar blades are out of the water. When feathered the blades are parallel to the surface of the water (with the face of the blades facing upwards) so that they meets less wind resistance and is able to slice through the air during the recovery. During the drive the wrists should be straight with the arms.

Feathering starts when the rower drops the hands to remove the blades from the water and most of the blades are out of the water. The rower rotates both wrists backwards as the arms are being extended. This will twist the oars such that the blades rotate from being perpendicular to being parallel to the surface of the water.

As the recovery phase completes, the rower squares the blades just as the hands are over the ankles. The wrists rotated forward to normal position to square the blades in readiness for the catch.

Rowing Physiology

Rowing is a sport of intense physical activity and this chapter gives some background on how the body functions to deliver the effort required. For a physical activity such as rowing the body should be trained for two levels of fitness, energy fitness and muscle fitness. Energy fitness relates to the delivery of energy to the muscles, and muscle fitness is the strength, flexibility and endurance of the muscles.

The energy that the body needs for rowing activity comes from the conversion of glucose in the form of glycogen within the cell into energy by a process called respiration. There two types of respiration: aerobic respiration and anaerobic respiration.

Aerobic Respiration

Aerobic respiration is firstly the transport of oxygen from outside the body to the cells within tissues of the body, and secondly it is the metabolic process by which oxygen reacts with glycogen in the cells to produce energy, water and carbon dioxide.

The transportation of oxygen involves three systems, the respiratory system, the circulatory system and the muscular system. The respiratory system involves the intake of oxygen into the lungs and then the diffusion of oxygen from the air through the walls of the tiny air sacs of the lungs into the blood. During exercise the lungs of a normal person can take in 120 to 180 liters of air per minute, while an elite rowing athlete can have an intake of over 200 liters of air per minute.

The circulatory system, consisting of the heart and the vascular system which carries the blood, saturated with oxygen, from the lungs to the heart where it is pumped through the arteries to the muscles of the body. Hemoglobin in the red blood cells actually carries the oxygen within the blood. Trained athletes generally have more total blood volume and a greater number of red blood cells than untrained persons. In the muscular system, oxygen diffuses through the walls of the capillaries into the muscle cells where it is used for the metabolic reaction with glucose in the form of glycogen to produce energy.

Rowers should strive to improve their level of conditioning by doing regular aerobic exercise.

Anaerobic Respiration

The body can also produce energy by anaerobic respiration and this occurs when the level of exertion is such that there is insufficient oxygen present for aerobic respiration to occur. This is called the anaerobic threshold and is the point at which anaerobic respiration starts to occur and glycogen is converted to energy and lactic acid without the use of oxygen. The presence of lactic acid causes muscle stiffness and cramping. Anaerobic respiration is much less efficient than aerobic respiration and produces only about 10% of the energy produced by aerobic respiration. Once the level of effort decreases such there is sufficient oxygen for the activity then any excess oxygen will recombine with lactic acid to reproduce the glycogen.

The body normally uses aerobic respiration for its energy needs, but when the body is engaged in intense physical activity the oxygen delivery to the cells may be insufficient for aerobic respiration to occur, so anaerobic respiration takes place. Anaerobic respiration occurs at the start of a sprint race as the rower's perform the initial set of power strokes and also during the final sprint at the end of the race, while aerobic respiration occurs during the distance phase of the race.

Regular training can make the body more efficient at aerobic respiration and prolong the onset of the anaerobic threshold.

In short sprint races about 70-80% of the energy used by a rower comes from aerobic respiration and 20-30% from anaerobic respiration. However, during longer head races approximately 90-95% of the energy will come from the aerobic system and 5-10% from the anaerobic system. Because of the high aerobic demand of head racing a good aerobic training is essential.

Breathing

Breathing correctly is vitally important while rowing because of the large amount of oxygen needed to generate energy for the muscles. A rower should have a regular breathing pattern during the stroke. There are two approaches to breathing for rowing: one has the lungs empty at the catch and the other has the lungs full of breath at the catch. For each of these approaches there are a couple of breathing patterns that can be used at different rowing speeds. For the full lung approach, the rower can use these breathing patterns:

1. One breath per stroke, exhaling on the drive and inhaling on the recovery. This is typically used for lower speeds.

2. Two breathes per stroke, exhaling on the drive, inhaling at the release and then exhaling during the recovery and inhaling at the catch. This would be used at higher speeds.

For the empty lung approach, the rower can use these breathing patterns:

1. One breath per stroke, inhaling on the drive and exhaling on the recovery. This is typically used for lower speeds.

2. Two breathes per stroke, inhaling on the drive, exhaling at the release and then inhaling during the recovery and exhaling at the catch. This would be used at higher speeds.

Taking shallow breaths makes it easier to control a rower's breathing. A novice rower should take guidance from their coach on which approach to use.

Muscles

Muscles are composed of muscle fibers which are cylindrical cells about 50-100 nanometers (nanometer is one billionth of a meter) in diameter and several centimeters long. The strength of an individual muscle fiber increases with its diameter, the greater its diameter the stronger the fiber is. These fibers arranged in parallel bundles along the length of the muscle. Individuals have the same number of muscle fibers within a particular muscle, and it is the diameter of the muscle fibers in their muscles that determines their strength.

Muscles contract when an electrical pulse is received from a nerve cell called a motor neuron attached to the muscle fiber. The muscle fiber responds to this electrical pulse by contracting momentarily. This short contraction and relaxation of the muscle fiber, called a twitch, lasts for 10-100 milliseconds. A single motor neuron and the fibers it stimulates are called a motor unit. One motor neuron may control from 2-2,000 muscle fibers.

For a stronger contraction another pulse must be received from the attached nerve cell before the first twitch subsides. For a sustained contraction a rapid series of pulses must be received by the muscle fiber. As a muscle fiber contracts it is constantly contracting and relaxing in response to a steady flow of electrical impulses from the nerve cell. A typical skeletal muscle has several hundred muscle fibers each with an attached nerve cell.

Most muscles contain a combination of two types of fibers:

- Slow-twitch (Type I) muscle fibers which respond more slowly and produce weaker contractions, but over a longer duration, and also have high aerobic capacity as they have a larger number of capillaries surrounding them.

- Fast-twitch (Type II) muscle fibers which respond more quickly with stronger contractions, but with a shorter duration, and also have high anaerobic capacity. These fibers are larger the slow-twitch muscles giving them the capability of stronger contractions.

Fast-twitch fibers tend to tire more quickly than slow-twitch fibers. Fast-twitch fibers are used to produce bursts of intense effort, while slow-twitch fibers are used for endurance. Fast-twitch fibers are mainly used for intense anaerobic activity, while slow-twitch fibers are used for aerobic activity. This means that to exercise fast-twitch fibers, high intensity training is required. Slow-twitch fibers are darker in color than fast-twitch fibers.

The average person has a roughly the same number of slow-twitch fibers and fast-twitch fibers. However, some individuals have either higher percentage of slow-twitch fibers or a higher percentage of fast-twitch fibers. Competitive rowers often have a higher percentage (70-85%) of slow-twitch fibers. Persons with a higher percentage of fast-twitch fibers tend to do better at sports such as sprinting that need short bursts of energy.

Bio-Mechanics of Rowing

Bio-mechanics refers to the muscles used during rowing. Rowing is a sport that uses all the major muscle groups of the body and also exercises multiple joints through a large range of motion in a non impact manner.

During the initial part of the drive the powerful quadriceps extend the knee. As the legs finish their extension, the hip is also extended by using the gluteus and hamstring muscles. The pivot of the back is done by the contraction of the erector spinae of the back.

As the arms start to pull the oar towards the chest, the biceps and brachialis in the upper arm and the brachioradialis in the forearm are engaged, as well as the upper body muscles including the latissimus dorsi, the rhomboid, the pectoralis major and the trapezius muscles. The posterior deltoid and teres minor muscles of the shoulder are also employed.

During the recovery, the triceps brachii and the anterior deltoids flex for the arms away position. The wrist extensors are used for the feathering action. The abdominals are used for the forward pivot of the torso. The gastrocnemius of the lower legs is engaged as the knee flexes for the forward movement of the seat.

Training

A good training program is needed for competitive rowing. The training should focus on improvement of rowing technique, cohesion of the crew, and the conditioning, strength and flexibility of the body. A training program will have these components:

- Type of training. This would include on the water rowing, on rowing machines, running, cycling, etc. The type of training also has the categories of slow, long distance training,

- Duration. This is the time spent on the whole workout, or part of a workout.

- Frequency of workouts. This is how often the workout is performed.

- Intensity of the workouts.

This book does not cover the schedules and details of a complete training program for rowing.

Drills

Drills are used to improve rowing technique and cohesion of the crew. There is a wide variety of drills to practice individual elements of the stroke and a few are described here. The same drill may be known by different names. The coach or the cox gives instructions and calls out the commands during the drill.

Square Blade Rowing

The strokes are done with the blade perpendicular to the water without feathering. This may be done in groups of rowers: pairs, fours, etc. The goal is to focus on blade placement at the catch and release.

Shoulder Pick

Start with arms only with the rower's backs in the finish position. Start to row with arms only. Do 20 of these arms only strokes.

Forward Pick

This is a standard warm-up drill for many crews. The goal is to exercise the different parts of the stroke. Start with arms only with the rower's backs in the finish position. Start to row with arms only as for the Shoulder Pick drill. After about 20 strokes, add the back motion. After a further 20 strokes, add leg motion to half slide. Finally after another 20 strokes, go to full slide motion.

Reverse Pick

The goal is to exercise the different parts of the stroke. Start with legs only with the rower's backs in the catch position and arms extended forward. After 20 strokes, add the back motion. After a further 20 strokes, add arm motion and row normally.

Quarter and Half Slide

The goal is to exercise quick catches for racing starts. Row quarter and half slide strokes at high power.

Cut the Cake

The goal is to improve balance. On the drive keep the oar out of the water and feathered and then continue as usual. Do this every third stroke.

Pause Drill

The goal is to improve balance. Pause for several seconds at the catch and then resume the stroke. This can also be done at the release. The cox will typically call "pause" and "row" to resume.

Acceleration

This is also known as the pair add-in drill. The goal is to feel the acceleration and the contribution from each pair in a boat. A selected pair starts to row at full slide. After 20 strokes the next pair adds in. This continues until all pairs are rowing. When the bow pair starts to row first, add in the other pairs in this order: stern pair, 3&4, 5&6. When 3&4 start to row first, add-in: bow pair, 5&6, stern pair. When 5&6 start to row first add in: 3&4, bow pair, stern pair.

Coxing

The coxswain is an important member of the crew. The coxswain is the leader of the crew on the water and has the following responsibilities:

- Safety and Management of the crew and boat in and out of the water.
- Steering the boat.
- Motivating the crew during the race.
- Make tactical decisions during the race.
- Organization and direction of the crew.
- Leading the crew through training drills.

A coxswain should also learn how to row. With this ability the coxswain will be able to offer feedback on any problems on stroke technique to other members of the crew.

The coxswain directs the crew using commands so that each member of the crew understands what is to be done, so that the same operation is executed by each crew member at the same time.

Crew and Boat Safety and Management

The safety and care of the crew and boat are of vital importance. Shells are fragile and dents and scratches are costly to repair. The coxswain should manage and direct the crew at all times to ensure that this is achieved. The coxswain should be aware of the conduct of the crew and control their activities from the time the boat is carried from the boathouse until it is returned to the boathouse.

Position

In eights the coxswain is always in the stern, while in coxed fours the coxswain may either be in the stern or the bow depending on whether shell is a stern-loader or a bow-loader. The coxswain should sit braced in the cockpit with feet on the foot boards and back on the back rest to avoid being slammed against the seat with each stroke. In a bow-loader the coxswain will be lying down in the bow cockpit of the boat.

Launching

The coxswain guides the crew as they carry the boat upside down to the dock. Before the boat is placed into the water the coxswain checks that the skeg is intact and the rudder is able to turn freely. The coxswain then calls "Roll/swing to water on two", "One, two", "Roll/swing", and the crew rolls the boat over to waist height, with each rower holding the starboard and port gunwales in each hand. On the command "Lower it in" the crew lowers the boat gently into the water. The coxswain ensures that the skeg and rudder are clear of dock. Once in the water, the coxswain puts the coxbox into the cockpit and holds a rigger while the crew get their oars.

The order in which the rowers and coxswain get into the boat varies by crew. For some crews it is coxswain first, then rowers, while for other crews it is rowers first and coxswain last. Once in the boat, the coxswain connects the coxbox to the loudspeaker cable and the head microphone connector, puts on the head microphone, turns on the coxbox and checks the audio over the loudspeakers. The coxswain now calls "Number off when ready" and each crew must call their seat number when ready. After the stroke seat has called, the coxswain should check that the direction of travel is clear and then call "Stroke/bow side push off".

Docking

On approaching the dock the boat should be lined up so that the port or starboard side of the boat will be positioned adjacent to the dock. Strokes by the stern pair will be sufficient to slowly move the boat towards the dock. When the bow reaches the dock the coxswain can call "Lean away", so the the crew leans away from the dock so that the oars and riggers can pass over the dock itself.

On return to the dock the coxswain leaves the boat first, followed by rowers with oars on the dock side and finally the rowers on the water side. When all the oars have been removed from the boat, it can be lifted from the water. To do so, the coxswain calls "Hands on", "Get ready to lift", "Lift and overhead".

Steering

The coxswain steers the boat and must know the intended course and direction of the boat and make steering adjustments as needed. Before a race the coxswain must become familiar with the course. The coxswain must get a copy of the course map and study it for location of the start and finish lines, stake boats and docks, the waiting area, the correct boat traffic direction, as well as any buoys, bridges, landmarks, currents, and other potential hazards. Ask a race official if anything is not clear.

Here is a typical course map.

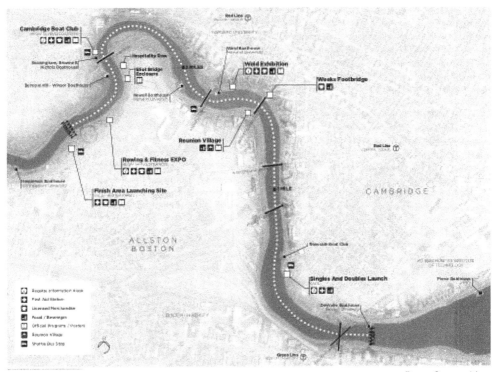

FORTY-SEVENTH **HEAD OF THE CHARLES REGATTA**   Race Course Map

Figure 48: Course Map

Correct steering in head races is important since these are normally on long winding riverine courses. The coxswain must steer a line that will minimize the time but also avoid any buoys and other riverside obstacles. The coxswain should take note of any landmarks when rowing to the starting line.

The coxswain should be aware of wind conditions. The coxswain will need to make small steering adjustments to counter a cross wind during a race. In the case of a cross wind a lane assignment that is on the lee side of other boats would have an advantage.

If the starting official asks the coxswain if the crew is ready, the cox should raise his hand briefly and have the crew sit ready to row.

At the end of the race the coxswain must make sure that the crew does not stop rowing until the boat has crossed the finished line.

Figure 49: Cox Box

Cox Box

A cox box provides the coxswain three primary functions:

- A stroke rate monitor. This lets the cox monitor the stroke throughout the race.

- An elapsed time counter. This used to measure elapsed time from the start of a race and also during training sessions.

- An electronic amplifier to broadcast commands to the rowers via speakers located throughout the shell. The coxswain has a head-mounted microphone which is plugged into the cox box. This ensures that each rower in an eight can clearly hear the coxswain's commands. Some cox boxes also have wireless capability so that the coach can also speak to the crew.

A cox box is usually used in eights and fours. The cox box is connected to two or three loudspeakers located throughout the shell as shown below. The cylindrical bracket for the cox box (shown in Figure 34) is mounted in the coxswain's cockpit. The cox box is inserted into the bracket and the connectors to the loudspeakers and the coxswain's head microphone must be plugged into it before use.

Figure 50: Speaker mounted in the cockpit

The coxswain should verify the cox box is charged before using it and when returning it make sure that it is plugged in so it will be charged before the next person uses it. Always carry the cox box by its strap and never carry it by the microphone or charger cord that plugs into it.

Commands

The coxswain uses commands to direct and manage crew activities both on and off the water. These include carrying the boat, rigging the boat, putting the boat into the water, race management and performing exercises and drills. Commands are not suggestions and the crew is expected to perform these commands when called by the coxswain. The commands given below are typical, individual crews may have other similar commands.

When giving commands it is important that they are clear, concise, confident and audible. The coxswain should be a good communicator saying just enough for the command to be easily understood. The crew may be in the middle of an activity like a power 10, lifting a boat, so each rower must able to immediately able to understand exactly what is required. Also the coxswain should vary the tone of his voice to keep the rowers concentrating and avoid monotone. Typically the commands should state the following items clearly:

- Instructions of what must be done: hands on, power 10, pressure, amount of slide, square/feather blades, etc.

- To whom is command directed: full crew, bow side, stroke side, bow four, stern pair, stern six, mid four, end pairs, etc.

- When to do it: either after a count until execution, or on the "Next stroke" at the catch.

- Execute the actual command with "Go".

To make sure that all crew members are present and ready to perform an operation such lifting a boat, the coxswain should a roll-call count down. The coxswain calls "Count down/number off from bow when ready" and each crew member must call their seat number when ready.

The timing of commands is important, so that the crew has sufficient time assimilate the command before acting on it. The coxswain should say "Go" at the release if the change to be made during the drive phase. The coxswain should say "Go" at the catch if the change to be made during the recovery phase.

Here are some examples of commands:

"Hands on", "One, two", "Lift"

"Power 10 in two", "One, two", "Go"

"Add stern pair in two", "One, two", "Stern pair in"

"Full pressure", "Next stroke", "Go"

"Roll to water in two", "One, two", "Go"

The coxswain should be consistent in the timing of the commands so that the crew gets used to when the command is to be performed. When the coxswain calls out strokes it should be done at the catch, the instant the stroke's blade enters the water.

Commands used out of the water

"Hands on". The rowers are to grab the gunwales of the boat in preparation to lift it overhead.

"Lift and bring it out". The rowers are to lift the boat and bring it out of the rack.

"Up and overhead". Together the rowers lift the shell overhead.

"Split to shoulder". The rowers take alternate sides of the shell and lower it to their shoulders before walking the shell to the water, or back to the boathouse.

"Roll/swing to water". The rowers roll the shell from the overhead position into the water.

Commands used on the water

"Hold water". Square the oars in the water to stop the boat immediately.

"Weigh enough" or "Easy". The crew stops whatever the current activity is.

"Let it run (glide)". The crew stops rowing at the release and lets the boat glide through the water and coast to a stop.

"Port (starboard) power up". The port or starboard rowers are to apply more power to their drives.

"Full pressure". The rowers are to apply maximum power during the drive.

"Light pressure". The rowers are to apply minimum power during the drive.

"Half pressure". The rowers are to apply medium power during the drive.

"Even pressure". The rowers are to apply equal power on both starboard and port sides.

"Add bow pair in x". The bow pair starts row in x strokes.

"Back it down". The rowers start backing strokes.

"7, back it down". The rower at seat 7 starts backing strokes.

"Bow, take a stroke". The bow rower takes a single stroke.

"Stern pair back x". The stern pair backs x strokes to turn the shell.

"Stern four back x". The stern four backs x strokes to turn the shell.

"Stern six back x". The stern six backs x strokes to turn the shell.

"Slow the slide" or "Adjust the ratio". To correct rushing the slide on the recovery.

"Port (starboard) to hold, starboard (port) to row. Ready to row. Row." To turn the boat.

Races and Regattas

In competitive rowing there are three different types of races: side-by-side sprints, head races and Bumps races. There are also different categories of race by type of boat and ability. For high school rowers these categories are:

- Junior-varsity boys
- Junior-varsity girls
- Varsity boys
- Varsity girls

For college and club rowers these categories are:

- Novice women
- Novice men
- Women
- Men

Side by Side Sprint Race

In a side by side sprint race all the boats start at the same time from a stationary position and race in separate lanes to the finish line. The winner is the boat that crosses the finish line first. The standard distance for these races is 2 kilometers or 1.5 kilometers for U.S. high school races. These races are typically held in the spring or summer. In this type of racing the term "boat length" is used to indicate how far ahead a boat is relative to another boat. The term "seat ahead" is used if the seat number N+1 of one boat is level with seat N of the other boat. When a boat is more than one length ahead it is referred to as open-water.

At the start of a sprint race all the boats line up side by side in their assigned lanes. The stern of each boat may be held by an official on a stake boat or a dock immediately behind the boat until the moment the race starts. If there is no starting dock, the starting official will give commands to the boats in the race to get them aligned.

Head Race

A head race is a timed race where the crews start at intervals of 10 to 20 seconds in order to avoid collisions and chase each other along the course. These races are typically on a river course over distances of between three and five miles. Boats begin with a moving start. The winner is the boat with the fastest time. The coxswain should steer the boat on a path that will minimize the time but also avoid any buoys and other riverside obstacles. Boats may be overtaken and the overtaken boat should steer out of the way and allow the overtaking boat to pass.

These races are typically held in the fall or early spring. There are several well-known head races:

- Head of the River Race over 4.25 miles on the river Thames in London.
- Head of the Charles race over 3.20 miles on the Charles River in Boston.
- Head of the Yarra race over 8.6 km on the Yarra River in Melbourne, Australia.
- Head of the Hooch over 5 km on the Tennessee River Chattanooga, Tennessee.
- Princeton Chase over 3 miles on Lake Carnegie, Princeton, New Jersey.
- Head of the Trent on the Trent-Severn Waterway in Peterborough, Ontario, Canada.
- Head of the Rideau in Ottawa, Ontario, Canada.
- Head of the Lake over 5 km through the Montlake Cut in Seattle, Washington.
- The Fremont 4-Miler in Seattle, Washington.
- Head of the Ohio over 3 miles on the Ohio river in Pittsburgh, Pennsylvania.
- Head of the Schuylkill over 3 miles in Philadelphia, Pennsylvania.
- Head of the Fish in Saratoga Springs, New York.
- Ringvaart Regatta over 100 km on the Ringvaart, a circular canal, in the Netherlands.

Bumps Race

A Bumps race is a series of races over several days. In each race a number of boats start at fixed intervals (about one and a half boat lengths) along a river and each crew attempts to catch and "bump" the boat in front and not be caught by the boat behind. Actual physical contact between the two boats is avoided and a "bump" is called when the bow ball of the chasing boat passes the coxswain of the chased boat.

The two crews involved in any bump then stop racing and pull into the bank to allow the rest of the boats to carry on. There are variations on this rule where the bumping crew pulls over but the bumped crew must continue racing over the entire course and can be bumped by more than one crew per day. A bumped crew starts the next race behind any of the boats that caught it. Bumps racing is typically done on a long, narrow stretch of river. Each year Cambridge University holds the Lent Bumps and May Bumps on the river Cam. The Town Bumps are held annually on the Isis river at Oxford in May.

Race Terminology

There is a standard way of naming the types of races. All races are named by an 'M' or 'W' for Men or Women followed by the number of rowers in the boat and then either a '+' or '-' to indicate a coxed or coxless sweep boat, or a 'x' to indicate a scull, For example: W8+ is a women's eight, M4- is a men's coxless four, M2x is a men's pair.

To denote a Lightweight race, the race name is prefixed with an 'L'. To denote a Junior (under 19) race the race name is prefixed with a 'J'. For example, LM8+ is a lightweight men's eight, JW8+ is a junior women's eight.

Olympic Races

Rowing has been an event in the Olympics since the 1900 Summer Olympics. Women's events were introduced at the 1976 Summer Olympics in Montreal. Lightweight rowing events were introduced to the games in 1996. The current Olympics have the following 14 events, all of them over a 2000 m side-by-side course of six lanes:

Men: Single Sculls, Double sculls, Quad sculls, Coxless pair, Coxless four, Eight

Lightweight Men: Double Sculls, Coxless Four

Women: Single Sculls, Double Sculls, Quad Sculls, Coxless Pair, Eight

Lightweight Women: Double Sculls

Repechage

Most rowing competitions (regattas) use repechage. Repechage is double elimination system in which each crew has a second chance to advance to the finals. It is an alternative to seeding. Usually only the first one or two boats in a heat will qualify automatically for the next round, and all of the other boats must race again in a second special heat known as the repechage to qualify. Competitors generally prefer double elimination because they get a second chance if they have been eliminated in a qualifying round for uncharacteristically poor performance.

Parts of a Race

A sprint race can be broken down into a sequence of stages.

- Racing start. This is a sequence of short strokes followed by a Power 10 at about 40 SPM to bring the boat up to speed as quickly as possible.

- Distance phase. The crew now settle to a steady cadence at about 32 SPM.

- Final sprint to the finishing line. The final sprint is fast and the rowers must give everything that they have and push themselves to their limits. Technique is not as important on the sprint. All that matters is getting over the line first.

During the race, the coxswain should keep the crew informed of the distance to the finish.

Starting Commands

For a sprint race the starting official will call the following commands:

1. "Rowers ready". The rowers move their seats to the catch position and put their squared blades into the water.

2. "Attention". Wait for the next command to start rowing.

3. "Row". The rowers start their first stroke.

Racing Start

The first strokes of a sprint race are the hardest because of the effort required to overcome the inertia of the boat and it usually takes at least three to four full strokes to get to race pace. It is more efficient to do a number of shorter, faster strokes that use only part of the slide range at the beginning of a race. The shorter strokes are named by the fraction of the distance the seat has travelled up the slide from the release position.

The 1/2-slide position is when the slide is at the halfway point in its range of travel. This is when the rower's knees are bent at a 90 degree angle. The 3/4-slide position is when the slide is 3/4 of the way from its stern-most position at the release. The legs are compressed to the point where the heels are almost off the footstretcher.

There are various short stroke sequences used for racing starts. The first stroke starts at the short stroke position.

3/4 - 1/2 - 3/4 - 3/4 - Full

3/4 - 1/2 - 1/2 - 3/4 - Full

3/4 - 1/2 - 3/4 - Full

1/2 - 1/2 - 3/4 - Full

Better power can be gained from the set of shorter strokes than from full strokes since the shorter strokes utilize the more powerful muscle groups in the legs and back to achieve a more rapid start. The sequence of short strokes is followed by a full stroke Power 10/20 at about 40 SPM. Next the crew should establish a steady cadence at about 30 SPM for the distance phase of the race.

Regattas

A rowing competition is called a regatta. Many boat racing regattas are held world-wide every year. These include regattas at every level: between school, club, university and national crews. Here is a sample of the more well-known:

Doggetts's Coat and Badge Race

The Doggett's Coat and Badge Race is the oldest single sculling race in the world. It has been raced since 1715 on the Thames from London Bridge to Cadogan Pier, Chelsea over a distance of four miles and five furlongs. Today it is raced in late July in single sculls. The prize is a traditional Watermen's red coat with a silver badge showing the horse of the House of Hanover and the word "Liberty".

See http://www.doggettsrace.org.uk/

The Boat Race

The Boat Race, raced annually by the rowing crews from Oxford and Cambridge University is one of the oldest sporting events in the world. The first race took place in 1829 at Henley on Thames. Since 1835 the race has been held in London. The current course is over 4.2 miles (6.8 km) on the tideway portion of the the Thames from Putney Bridge to Chiswick Bridge at Mortlake. Although the course is upstream, the race is timed to start with the incoming tide to ensure that the crews have the fastest possible current. Cambridge has won 81 times, Oxford 77 times and there has been one dead heat.

See http://theboatrace.org/

The Head of the River Race

The Head of the River Race is held annually on the River Thames in London from Mortlake to Putney over 4.25 miles. This race is held on the ebb tide. This is a head race open to men's eights with over 400 competing crews. The race was started in 1925 by the rowing coach Steve Fairbairn.

See http://www.horr.co.uk/

Henley Royal Regatta

Henley Royal Regatta, first held in 1839, is a rowing event held annually on the River Thames at Henley-on-Thames. The regatta lasts for five days over the first weekend in July. The races are head-to-head knock out competitions in which two boats compete over a course of 1 mile, 550 yards. This is 112 meters longer than the standard international competition distance of 2000 meters. Heats are held on the first four days with the finals on the last day. This regatta attracts crews from all over the world.

See http://www.hrr.co.uk/

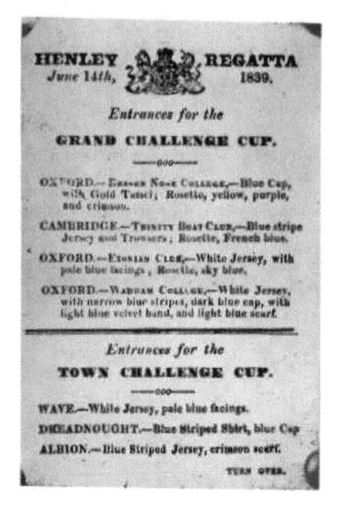

Figure 51: Henley Regatta Poster 1839

BUCS Rowing Regatta

The British Universities and College Sports rowing regatta, held in Nottingham, Great Britain is the largest regatta in Europe with over 7000 crews competing. This is a 2000 meter side by side sprint regatta.

The Great Race

The Great Race is held on the Waikato River over a 3.84 km upstream course from Ann St. Reserve to Ferry Bank Park in Hamilton, New Zealand. The race is between the men's eights from the University of Waikato and well known university crews from outside New Zealand. In recent years the Melbourne, Cambridge, Oxford and Harvard universities have been competitors.

See http://www.thegreatrace.co.nz/

The Head of the Charles

The Head of the Charles is held annually on the last weekend in October on the Charles river that separates Boston and Cambridge. It is a head race over 3.2 miles from the Charles river basin to the Eliot bridge. It is the largest two-day regatta in the world with over 9000 athletes competing.

See http://hocr.org/

Dad Vail Regatta

The Dad Vail Regatta has been in existence since 1934. Today it is the largest regular intercollegiate rowing regatta in the U.S. and is held annually on the Schuylkill River in Philadelphia, Pennsylvania. The regatta is named for "Dad" Vail who coached at the University of Wisconsin-Madison for many years. Over a hundred colleges from the United States and Canada compete.

Yale-Harvard Boat Race

The Yale-Harvard Boat Race has been held annually on the Thames River, New London, Connecticut since 1859.The race, which was first raced in 1852, is America's oldest collegiate athletic competition. Since 1876 it has been raced over 4 miles. Currently there are three events on race day: the 2 mile freshmen race, the 3 mile junior varsity race and the 4 mile varsity race. To date Harvard has had 93 wins and Yale 54 wins.

IRA Championship Regatta

The Intercollegiate Rowing Association holds the IRA Championship Regatta, which is considered to be the United States collegiate national championship of rowing. It is held on the Cooper River in Pennsauken, New Jersey.

Eastern Sprints

The Eastern Sprints is the annual rowing championship for the Eastern Association of Rowing Colleges (EARC) and have been held since 1946. The race is held on Lake Quinsigamond in Worcester, Massachusetts in May. These are 2000 m races. Teams include the Ivy League universities as well as Georgetown University, Syracuse University, U.S. Naval Academy, MIT, BU, Rutgers, Northeastern, Wisconsin, and George Washington University.

Royal Canadian Henley Regatta

The Royal Canadian Henley Regatta has been held annually since 1880. It has been hosted at Martindale Pond, Port Dalhousie, St. Catherines, Ontario in August.

See http://www.henleyregatta.ca/

International Huegel Regatta

The International Huegel Regatta on Lake Baldeney in Essen, Germany is a large European regatta with competitors for around the world.

Coupe de la Jeunesse

The Coupe de la Jeunesse is an international junior regatta with 2000 m races held annually at various locations in Europe.

See http://www.couperowing.org/

Clubs and Associations

Rowing is performed at several different levels: high schools, clubs and universities. Many countries have rowing associations at the national level.

Rowing Club Argentino

This is the national rowing club in Argentina.

http://rowingclubargentino.com.ar/

British Rowing Association

British Rowing is the governing body for the sport of rowing in Great Britain.

http://www.britishrowing.org/

Rowing Australia

Rowing Australia is the national governing body for the sport of rowing in Australia. It holds the following national regattas: Australian Rowing Championships, Australian Masters Championships, Youth Cup and Australian Youth Olympic Festival.

http://www.rowingaustralia.com.au/

Austria Rowing Association / Oesterreichscher Ruderverband

This is the national rowing association in Austria.

http://www.rudern.at/

Rowing Canada

Rowing Canada Association is the national governing body for the sport of rowing in Canada.

http://www.rowingcanada.org/

Canadian University Rowing Association

Canadian University Rowing Association (CURA) is the governing body for rowing at universities in Canada and organizes the annual championship regatta.

Czech Rowing Association

The Czech Rowing Association is the national governing body for rowing in the Czech Republic.

http://www.veslovani.cz/

Danish Rowing Federation

The Danish Rowing Federation is the national governing body for rowing in Denmark.

http://www.roning.dk

FISA

FISA, the International Rowing Federation, is the governing body for international rowing, established in 1892. FISA started the World Rowing Championships in 1962. This week long event, is currently held annually at different venues around the world. Men's lightweight and Women's open weight events were added to the championships in 1974.

http://www.worldrowing.com

German Rowing Association / Deutscher Ruderverband

Deutscher Ruderverband is the national governing body for the sport of rowing in Germany.

http://www.rudern.de/

Hellenic Rowing Federation

http://www.kopilasia.gr/

Rowing Federation of India

Rowing Federation of India is the national rowing association in India.

http://www.indiarowing.com/

Rowing Ireland

Rowing Ireland governs the sport of rowing in Ireland.

http://www.iaru.ie/

Italian Rowing Federation / Federazione Italiana Canottaggio

Federazione Italiana Canottaggio is the national body of rowing in Italy.

http://www.canottaggio.org

New Zealand Rowing Association

The New Zealand Rowing Association (NZRA) is the governing body of rowing in New Zealand.

http://rowingnz.com/

Scottish Rowing

Scottish Rowing governs the sport of rowing in Scotland.
http://www.scottish-rowing.org.uk/

Societe Havraise de l'Aviron

http://www.avironlehavre.org/

Rowing South Africa

Rowing South Africa governs the sport of rowing in South Africa.
http://www.rowsa.co.za/

Spanish Rowing Federation

Spanish Rowing Federation is the orgaizing body for rowing in Spain.
http://www.federemo.org/

Row Sweden

Row Sweden governs the sport of rowing in Sweden.
http://www.algonet.se/

Swiss Rowing Federation

Swiss Rowing Federation is the national association for rowing in the Switzerland.
http://www.ruderverband.ch/

US Rowing

USRowing is the national association for rowing in the USA.
http://www.usrowing.org/

Welsh Rowing

Welsh Rowing is the governing body for the sport of rowing in Wales.
http://www.welshrowing.com

Further Reading

Books

Here is a list of books that provide more information on rowing.

Boyne, Daniel J. 2000. *Essential Sculling*, The Globe Pequot Press

Bourne, Gilbert C. 1925. *A Textbook of Oarsmanship*, Oxford University Press

Davenport, Mike, 2002. *The Nuts and Bolts Guide to Rigging*, SportWork, Inc.

Halberstam, David. 1985. *The Amateurs*, William Morrow and Company, Inc.

Keisling, Steven. 1982. *The Shell Game*, William Morrow and Company, Inc.

Keisling, Steven. 1990. *The Complete Recreational Rower & Racer*, Crown Publishers, Inc.

McArthur, John. 1997. *High Performance Rowing*, The Crowood Press, Ltd.

Nolte, Victor. (Ed.), 2011. *Rowing Faster*, Human Kinetics, Inc.

Paduda, Joe. 1992. *The Art of Sculling*, Ragged Mountain Press

Simon, Laura; Zalkind, Margot; Stokes, Stew. 2009, *The Coxswain Encyclopedia*, The Foundation for Rowing Education, Inc.

The International Rowing Federation. 2002. *The FISA Coaching Development Program Handbook*, FISA

Web Sites

Here is some web sites that will provide you with information on rowing:

Rowing Clubs and Associations

World Rowing http://www.worldrowing.com/

row2k http://www.row2k.com/

Rowing Links http://www.rowinglinks.com

Friends of Rowing History http://www.rowinghistory.net/

World Rowing Magazine http://www.worldrowingmagazine.com

River and Rowing Museum, Henley http://rrm.co.uk/

Rowing Instruction

Black Bear Sculling http://www.blackbearsculling.com/

Calm Waters Rowing http://www.calmwatersrowing.net/

Craftsbury Sculling Camps
http://www.craftsbury.com/sculling/camps/home.htm

The Florida Rowing Center http://www.floridarowingcenter.com/

Boat and Equipment Manufacturers

Adirondack Rowing http://www.adirondackrowing.com/

Concept2 http://www.concept2.com/

Coxmate http://www.coxmate.com.au/

Croker Oaks http://www.crokeroars.com/

Durham Boat Company http://www.durhamboat.com

Empacher http://empacher.de/

Filippi Elite Rowing http://www.eliterowing.com/

Hudson Boat Works https://www.hudsonboatworks.com/

Kaschper Racing Shells http://www.kaschper.com/

Maas Boat Company http://maasboats.com/

Nielsen-Kellerman http://nkhome.com//

Peinert Boatworks http://www.peinert.com/

Pocock Racing Shells http://www.pocock.com/
Resolute Racing Shells http://www.resoluteracing.com/
Vespoli Racing Shells http://www.vespoli.com/
Virginia Rowing Company http://www.virginiarowing.com/

Regattas

The Boat Race http://theboatrace.org/
Doggetts's Coat and Badge Race http://www.doggettsrace.org.uk/
The Head of the Charles http://hocr.org/
Henley Royal Regatta http://www.hrr.co.uk/
The Royal Canadian Henley Regatta http://www.henleyregatta.ca/
San Diego Crew Classic http://crewclassic.org/
Head of the Schuylkill Regatta http://www.hosr.org/
Head of the Yarra http://www.headoftheyarra.com/
Rowing World Lucerne http://www.ruderwelt-luzern.ch/
The Great Race http://www.thegreatrace.co.nz/

Glossary

Rowing has its own unique terminology.

Backstay

This is the part of a rigger that goes from the top of the oarlock to the gunwale of the shell. This helps to brace the rigger and connect it to the hull.

Backstop

The stop mechanism on the seat slides to prevent the seat from coming off the tracks at the bow end.

Blade

This is the wide, flat part of the oar that goes into the water.

Bow

This is the forward section of the boat and the first part of the boat to cross the finish line.

Bow Ball

The rubber ball at the end of the bow to prevent damage to people or shells.

Bow coxed boat

A shell in which the coxswain is near the bow instead of the stern. It is hard to see the coxswain in this type of boat, because only his head is visible. Having the coxswain virtually lying down in the bow reduces wind resistance, and the weight distribution is better.

Button

A wide collar on the oar that keeps it from slipping through the oarlock.

Catch

The point in the stroke at which the oar blade is placed into the water. This marks the beginning of the drive and the end of the recovery.

Catch angle

The catch angle is the oar angle at the catch position. See oar angle.

CLAM

Clip-on Load Adjustment Method. This is a shim that clips over the sleeve of an oar on the outboard side of the collar to reduce the gearing or load of an oar.

Cockpit

The part of the boat in which the rowers sit.

Collar

See Button.

Course

A straight area of a body of water, typically four to eight lanes wide, marked with buoys for rowing competitions. An Olympic course is 2000 meters. High school races are usually 1500 meters. A head race has a much longer course (three miles or more) usually following a winding river.

Coxswain

This is the person who steers the shell and directs the crew. Also called the cox'n or cox.

Cox box

A battery-operated electronic device that includes a digital stroke rate monitor, an elapsed time readout and a voice amplifier. The coxswain uses the cox box to monitor the race and to make his or her commands more audible to the crew. The coxswain typically wears a head-mounted microphone, which is connected to the cox box.

Crab, or Catch a Crab

This occurs at the end of a drive when an oar gets stuck below the water and it is difficult to get out. This can lead to the rower getting ejected from the boat.

Crossover

In sculling, this is when the one oar handle crosses over the other handle during the drive and recovery.

Drive

That portion of the stroke when the blades are in the water and the rower is pulling on the oar handles.

Deck

The part of the shell at the bow and stern that is covered with fiberglass cloth or thin plastic.

Engine room

The biggest and strongest rowers in the middle seats in the boat. In an eight, these are seats 3, 4, 5 and 6.

Ergometer

Also called a rowing machine or "erg". It simulates the actual rowing motion and is used for training.

Feathering

The act of twisting the oar to position the blade vertically for the drive and horizontally for the recovery.

FISA

Federation Internationale des Societes d'Aviron (International Federation of Rowing Societies). The international governing body for the sport of rowing in the world, established in 1892.

Frontstop

A stop at stern end of the track that the rower's seat slides on. The wheels of the seat should almost reach the frontstop at the catch of each stroke.

Gate

The bar across the oarlock that keeps the oar in place.

German rigging

A different way of setting up which side of the boat the oars are on in a sweep boat. Instead of alternating from side to side all the way down, in a German rigged boat, two consecutive rowers have oars on the same side.

Grips

Rubber caps on the inboard (handle) end of the oars.

Gunwale

The upper edge of the hull to which the riggers are bolted. Pronounced "gun-el".

Head Race

This is a timed race where the crews start at intervals and chase each other along the course.

Heat

A qualifying race within a specific race category. For example, men's varsity eight (MV8).

Heavyweight

The weight class in men's rowing for rowers over the lightweight restriction.

Hull

The external body of the shell.

Inboard

The distance from the butt of oar handle to the inside edge side of the collar.

Inside hand

The sweep boat rower's hand that is closest to the rigger. The sweep boat rower uses the inside hand to feather the oar. When rowing at port, the right hand is the inside hand, and when rowing at starboard the left hand is the inside hand.

Layback

The amount of reverse pivot of a rower's torso from the hips during the last third of the drive for a proper finish position.

Lightweight

A racing category that refers to the bodyweight of the rowers. Under current rules, the Lightweight class weight limits are 150 pounds for boys and 130 pounds for girls.

Novice

A rower in his or her first rowing season, without regard for academic grade level. Novice high school rowers are usually freshmen or sophomores.

Oar

Used to drive the boat forward: rowers do not use paddles.

Oar angle

The oar angle is between the oarshaft and a line perpendicular to the centerline axis of the shell.

Oarlock

This is a U-shaped plastic bracket that holds the oar and swivels on the pivot pin, which is mounted at the end of the rigger. Also called a row-lock.

Orthogonal Position

When the oar is perpendicular to the longitudinal axis of the shell.

Outboard/outside hand

The sweep boat rower's hand that holds the oar handle furthest from the rigger. When rowing at port the left arm is the outside arm, and when rowing at starboard the right arm is the outside arm.

Petite Final

This is the final for boats that were eliminated from the final.

Pin

The metal peg that forms the pivot for the oarlock.

Port

Left side of the boat, while facing forward, in the direction that the boat is moving.

Power 10 or 20

Coxswain's command for the rowers to do ten/twenty of their best, most powerful strokes.

Quarter-slide, half-slide, three-quarter-slide and full slide

Distances of the slide from the sternmost (release) position.

Ratio

This is the ratio of the time taken for the drive and the time taken for the recovery portion of the stroke. The ideal ratio should be about 0.5, meaning that twice as much time is taken during the recovery as compared with the drive.

Recovery

That part of the stroke when the blades are out of the water and the person is moving towards the next drive.

Regatta

A boat racing meet with a several races. A high school regatta may have races in the following men's and women's classes, for four- and eight-seat boats: varsity, junior varsity (JV), lightweight, freshman, and novice.

Release

That point at which the oars are taken out of the water at the end of the drive, also the beginning of the recovery.

Repechage

The second-chance race which ensures that everyone has two chances to advance from preliminary races since there is no seeding in the heats.

Rigger

The triangular metal arm that extends from the side of the boat to which the oarlock is attached.

Rudder

The metal or carbon fiber plate that pivots at the skeg at the aft-end of the keel and is controlled by the coxswain to steer the boat by attached cables.

Rudder Lines

Strings the coxswain uses to move the rudder and turn the shell.

Run

The run is the distance the shell moves during one stroke. This can be seen by looking at the distance between the puddles made by the same oar.

Rush the slide

Refers to moving the seat from the release position to the catch position too quickly.

Sax board

Another name for the gunwale.

Sculling

The discipline of rowing where scullers use two oars or sculls. Singles (one rower), doubles (two rowers) and the quads (four rowers) are sculls.

Sculler

A rower that uses two oars.

Set

The stability and balance of a shell.

Settle

The part of the race when the crew decreases the rating from the initial high stroke to a lower pace that the crew will maintain until the final sprint.

Shell

Another name for a boat.

Skeg

The fin attached to the keel of the shell that helps stabilize the shell and maintain a straight course.

Skying

The blade being too high above the water at the end of the catch.

Sleeve

Plastic tube on the oar, under the button, that protects against wear in the oarlock.

Slide

The set of two runner tracks for the wheels of each underneath each seat in the boat.

Sling

This is a portable folding boat holder. Two are required to hold a boat.

Span

Distance from the center of starboard sculling oarlock pin to the center of the port oarlock.

Spin the boat

Turn the boat around to face the other direction.

Spread

Distance from the centerline of the shell to the center of the oarlock pin.

Sprint

The last part of a race, where boats make a final push in power and stroke rate to cross the finish line. Usually done in the last 250-500 meters.

Starboard

Right side of the boat, while facing forward, in the direction of movement.

Starboard-rigged

A shell rigged so that the stroke seat is a starboard rower.

Stern

The rear of the boat. The rowers face the stern.

Stern pitch

Aft slant on the blade when the oar is square in the water.

Straight

Refers to a shell without a coxswain i.e. a straight four or straight pair.

Stretcher or Footstretcher

The stretcher consists of two inclined footrests that hold the rower's shoes. The rower's shoes are attached to the footrests.

Stroke

The rower who sits closest to the stern. The stroke sets the pace for the other rowers.

Stroke rate

The number of strokes a crew takes in one minute, also called strokes per minute (SPM). Calculate the stroke rate by counting the number of strokes taken in 15 seconds and then multiply by 4.

StrokeCoach

A small electronic display that the coxswain can attach in the boat to show the important race information like stroke rate and elapsed time. Also called a cox box.

Sweep

The type of rowing where rowers use only one oar. Pairs (two rowers), fours (four rowers) and the eight are sweep boats. Pairs and fours may or may not have a coxswain. Eights always have a coxswain.

Swing

This is when the entire crew is moving perfectly in unison and the shell seems to be moving very fast without much effort.

Work-through the Pin

The amount by which the front of the rower's seat moves further sternward from a line between the oarlock pins.

Washing out

Not getting the blade deep enough into the water so that the blade comes out of the water too early.

Way-enough or Weigh-enough

Coxswain's command to stop rowing.

CPSIA information can be obtained
at www.ICGtesting.com
Printed in the USA
FSHW012244070120
65858FS

9 781495 350283